Bygone Dundee

Bernard Byrom

A view of the city centre and docks, taken from the top of the Steeple Church, commonly known as the Old Steeple. Much of the foreground remains recognisable today, with Whitehall Street emerging from between the two domed buildings onto the High Street, but the jumble of old buildings immediately beyond them would soon be swept away to build the Caird Hall and lay out the City Square. Earl Grey Dock is on the right of the Royal Arch and King William IV Dock is on the left, with a small paddle steamer (probably one of the Tay ferries) just visible in its graving dock. The large dock beyond the sheds is Victoria Dock while beyond that is Camperdown Dock. The Eastern Wharves occupy the land for some distance beyond the docks while the coastline in the distance curves round to Broughty Ferry whose castle can be seen prominently on the headland.

Stenlake Publishing Ltd

Text © Bernard Byrom, 2024.
First published in the United Kingdom, 2024, reprinted 2025,
by Stenlake Publishing Ltd.,
54-58 Mill Square,
Catrine, Ayrshire,
KA5 6RD

Telephone: 01290 551122
www.stenlake.co.uk

ISBN 9781840339710

Printed by:
P2D,
1 Newlands Road,
Westoning,
MK45 5LD

**The publishers regret that they cannot supply
copies of any pictures featured in this book.**

Acknowledgements

The author would like to thank the staff of Dundee Central Library for their assistance during the research of this book.

Further Reading

The following were the principal books and websites used by the author during his research:

Eric Eunson and Bill Early: *Old Dundee*, 2002

Francis H. Groome: *Ordnance Gazetteer of Scotland*, 1882

Brian King: *Dundee Through Time*, 2014

Charles McKean, Patricia Whatley and Kenneth Baxter: *Lost Dundee: Dundee's Lost Architectural Heritage*

Peter Waller: *Lost Tramways of Scotland: Dundee*

Scottish Post Office Directories: Dundee 1809-1950

Dundee Courier

Dundee Evening News

Dundee Evening Telegraph

Canmore: canmore.org.uk

Historic Environment Scotland: historicenvironment.scot

Leisure and Culture Dundee: leisureandculturedundee.com

Scottish Brewing Heritage: scottishbrewingheritage.org

Taymara: taymara.org

The Municipal History of Dundee (1878): tradeshouselibrary.org

The Unicorn Preservation Society: www.frigateunicorn.org.

findmypast.co.uk

Introduction

The city of Dundee, situated on the north bank of the mighty River Tay, had been granted the status of a royal burgh by 1191 but suffered repeated attacks over the next few centuries, initially from the English forces of King Edward I, the 'Hammer of the Scots', in the Wars of Independence (1296-1303). Its recovery from this was swift: the town became a prosperous seaport and in 1325 King Robert the Bruce granted Dundee the right to erect its first tollbooth and two years later he granted another charter to the town, the original one having been burnt by the English invaders. But it was not to last: in 1385 Dundee was again sacked and burned, this time by the forces of King Richard II of England. In 1547 it was captured by the English in the course of King Henry VIII's campaign of 'Rough Wooing' in his attempt to marry his son Edward (later King Edward VI) to the infant Mary, Queen of Scots; this time it took four years before the English were eventually driven out by a French force who then burned the town! Finally in 1651, after the town had been unwise enough to support King Charles II's unsuccessful bid to succeed his father, Oliver Cromwell sent General Monck to besiege the town. The siege lasted eight days and was followed by the town being torched once again, many of the buildings lying in ruins for decades.

In between these events the town recovered and prospered because it was able to resume importing and exporting goods and to resume manufacturing goods for its own consumption during more settled times. The 'trades' history dates back to 1124, when laws were passed for the regulation of various trades, and these regulations laid down standards to control prices and quality. From 1306, the trades were recognised as separate corporate bodies. But it soon became clear that they needed to act as a single body, and so the Nine Incorporated Trades of Dundee was set up as early as 1581. The nine trades consisted of the Baxters (bakers), Cordiners (shoemakers), Skinners (glovers), Tailors, Bonnetmakers, Fleshers (butchers), Hammermen (metalworkers), Weavers and Dyers.

Samuel Bell (1739-1813) became the burgh's architect during the 1770s and was responsible for several new civic buildings including St Andrew's Kirk in 1772, the Trades Hall in 1776, the English (Episcopalian) Chapel in 1782 and the Steeple Church in 1791. He also laid out St Andrew's Street in 1774, Crichton Street in 1777, Tay Street in 1793 and Castle Street in 1795. But matters were very different nearer the river. King William IV dock wasn't completed until 1825, followed by Earl Grey dock in 1834. Shore Terrace and Dock Street only extended as far eastward as Castle Street, all to the eastward being occupied as shipbuilding and timber yards. The buildings now forming the north side of Dock Street are built on what was then the bed of the river. The shoreline ran along behind the garden walls of the houses on the south side of the Nethergate and the whole space constituting West Dock Street and westward to South Lindsay Street was covered by the tide and formed part of the West Tide Harbour. Constitution Road was only a horse track, bounded on both sides by hedges enclosing market gardens. The area was finally claimed from the river and built up from the mid 1840s, when the Dundee & Perth Railway reclaimed land from the foreshore to build its line. This created a space between the railway and the town which was used to create the Esplanade and land westwards of it.

In the first half of the nineteenth century Dundee was the linen centre of the United Kingdom as well as becoming a centre for railways, engineering and associated industries. Its docks expanded to cope not only with the whaling fleet, the later herring fleet, and with an enormous increase in shipbuilding, but also with the huge clippers that travelled directly between Calcutta and Dundee, bringing in jute and returning to India and other parts of the world with manufactured linen goods and jute products. Jute became the main import of the town around 1858 and large-scale industry lay in a thick swathe around the fringes of the town. This industrial area, in which it became possible to count up to 200 factory chimneys, was the dominant characteristic of the town that became known as Juteopolis. The manufacturing of jute created a huge demand for whale oil, as this was used to soak the jute fibres before they were spun into cloth, and the city became the premier British whaling port. Its population grew from around 30,500 to 153,000 between 1820 and 1890, much of it living in the squalid conditions of run-down tenements.

By 1871 Dundee, although being the third largest town, had the largest surviving medieval town centre in Scotland. The result of the passing of the 1871 Improvement Act was to wipe away most of the squalid seventeenth and eighteenth century closes of the central area and replace them with the Victorian city centre which remained virtually intact until the middle of the twentieth century. The 1871 Act gave the town such new streets as Whitehall Crescent, Commercial Street and Victoria Road, and also saw the reconstruction of the Murraygate. Queen Victoria granted Dundee city status in 1889.

Jute production began to decline as early as the 1890s and, although boosted by the need for sandbags in the First World War, it continued its downward path thereafter as plastics became more popular. So, between the two World Wars, Dundee was characterised principally by industrial decline and suburban growth, with suburbs extending to the north and east and with the construction of the pioneering Logie housing estate in the north-west in 1918. The middle classes moved out to the west, to Broughty Ferry and Newport, so the centre of the city was left with decaying slums. To rejuvenate the city it was decided that the Vault, the Town House and associated buildings, should be demolished to make way for a new City Chambers and City Square. Work began in 1914 with the laying of the foundation stone of the Caird Hall and ended with the City Square complex which was completed in 1933. In Dundee's post-war Development Plan, published in 1952, only twelve buildings were considered worth protecting - seven of them churches and nothing in the Overgate - and everything else was considered to be expendable. The city centre was to be reshaped by a traffic bypass to which the promised Tay Road Bridge would be connected on former dockland at the very centre of town. The construction of the Inner Ring Road in the 1960s meant the final and largest clearance of medieval Dundee - the destruction of the vast swathe of the old city that had survived in and around the Overgate which was to be replaced by the first modern shopping centre of its type of Britain. The Overgate Centre was opened in the mid 1960s but within 37 years it had become run-down and unfashionable, particularly after the Wellgate Centre was opened in 1978. It was largely demolished, rebuilt and reopened in 2000. A major redevelopment of the waterfront was begun in 2001 and is still in progress; the centrepiece of this is the V&A Dundee, which opened next to Discovery Point in 2018.

In this early 1930s view the docks are empty and the Royal Arch is almost obscured by the vast bulk of the Caird Hall, a 2,300-capacity venue hosting live music, comedy, and classical music programmes. The hall was designed by the city architect James Thomson and the foundation stone was laid by King George V in 1914, but the First World War delayed its completion and it was formally opened by his son, Edward, Prince of Wales, in 1923. The new City Square, which can be seen on the left of the photograph flanked by new buildings and stretching down to the High Street, was opened in 1933.

When Queen Victoria and Prince Albert visited Dundee in 1844, it was decided to build a triumphal arch to mark the occasion. Time was too short to build one of stone so instead a rather plain wooden arch was erected in time for the visit. A competition was subsequently held for designing a permanent sandstone monument and this was won by John Thomas Rochead, who also designed the Wallace Monument near Stirling. Known as the Royal Arch or Victoria Arch and erected between 1849 and 1853, it cost upwards of £2,270 to build (around £240,000 in today's money), raised between public subscription and the harbour trustees. The arch was demolished in 1964 as part of land reclamation work required for the construction of the Tay Road Bridge. The event shown here was a Collection Day for the Royal Navy Lifeboat Institution (RNLI) on 2 June 1906.

The King William IV Dock and the West Graving Dock were built between 1812 and 1825 by Thomas Telford. Access was gained from the river through the Tidal Harbour which also gave access to the adjacent Earl Grey Dock. This view is looking west over the King William IV Dock. The buildings in the background are in Greenmarket (on the immediate right of the arch) and Dock Street (further to the right). The Royal Arch itself stands on the pier between the King William IV and Earl Grey Docks, with the Number 4 storage shed to the left.

A view of part of King William IV Dock, with Dock Street behind and Commercial Street entering it on the right. Three Caledonian Railway goods wagons are standing on the dockside opposite the end of Commercial Street with two more standing alongside the ketch. The premises of George Morton Limited, Distillers, Blenders, Wine and Whisky Merchants, take centre stage in this picture with the tower of St Paul's Episcopal Cathedral rising above its roofline. The dock was filled in for the Tay Road Bridge and its approaches.

Two paddle-wheel pleasure steamers are moored in King William IV Dock, with the Royal Arch prominent near the centre of the picture. From left to right, the prominent towers in the background are Dundee West Railway Station, the spire of St Paul's Meadowside Church, St Mary's Tower with its battlements, and the Town House and clock face.

The Earl Grey Dock was completed in 1834. The corner of Greenmarket is visible in the background and the church tower belongs to St Paul's Episcopal Cathedral. In the 1960s the dock, together with its associated buildings, vanished under the landfall of the Tay Road Bridge. The white steel-screw steamship is the *Thistle*, which was built in 1884. After working on the River Tay as a pleasure steamer for twenty years she was sold to a German company in 1905.

This is the Harbourmaster's Office and Observation Tower, situated by the lock (running in the foreground across the picture) at the entrance to Earl Grey Dock (out of picture to the left) from the Tidal Harbour, which is where the fishing boats on the right are lying. The tall-masted ships beyond are lying in the King William IV Dock.

Victoria Dock in 1902, with the sailing clipper on the left moored adjacent to the entrance to the graving dock. The two steam vessels on the other side of the dock have obviously discharged their cargoes because they are sitting high in the water. The ethereal background shows the domed building of the Sailors' Home while the tower of St Paul's Episcopal Cathedral soars above the city.

The Tay Ferries, known locally as the 'Fifies', were the main means of crossing the Tay with a vehicle until the opening of the Tay Road Bridge. Before 1713 unregulated ferries had provided an irregular service, but that year the Guildry of Dundee established a more reliable service between Dundee and Ferryport-on-Craig on the Fife coast. The sailing boats and pinnaces employed remained privately owned until the service passed into the control of the Tay Ferry Trustees in 1819; the service later came under the jurisdiction of the Dundee Harbour Trustees in 1870. The first regular scheduled steam-powered ferry started in 1821 when the *Union* ran six days a week with up to eleven crossings per day. Ferryport-on-Craig's harbour terminus was opened in 1848. The name was shortened to Tayport in 1851 so it could fit onto the tickets.

The ferryboat in the picture is the PS *Dundee*, which had the distinction of being the only paddle-wheel ferryboat to work the route. Seen here around 1910, she lasted until 1917. As early as 1921 Dundee Town Council proposed a road bridge across the Tay because of bottlenecks at the piers but in 1939 an additional ferry boat was decided upon as the cheaper option. A further ferryboat was added in 1951. The boats would typically carry ten vehicles at a time and their final crossings were made on 18 August 1966, the day the road bridge opened.

The Tay Rail Bridge can be seen in the background. In the 1870s a bridge carrying a single line of rails was designed by the engineer Thomas Bouch and was opened on 1 June 1878. The following year Queen Victoria travelled over the bridge on her return from Balmoral and rewarded Bouch with a knighthood. But disaster happened on 28 December the following year when the central section of the bridge, known as the High Girders, collapsed while a train was crossing during a furious storm. The High Girders and the train fell into the river; there were no survivors and around 75 lives were lost (the exact number was unknown). At the public enquiry the Commissioner for Wrecks concluded that the bridge had been 'badly designed, badly constructed and badly maintained' and put most of the blame on Bouch. His health and reputation broken, he died the following year. The bridge was dismantled and the stumps of its piers, seen in the picture, remain to this day. Work on a second bridge began in March 1882, 59 feet upstream and parallel to the old bridge. Designed by William Henry Barlow and built by William Arrol & Company of Glasgow, it was opened on 11 June 1887. During 2003 the bridge was strengthened and refurbished, and 1,100 tons of bird droppings were removed from the iron latticework.

This steam-hauled patent slip was designed by James Leslie and constructed in 1837 at the Panmure Shipyard on the Dundee waterfront. The 545-foot ramp shows the large dimensions of ships that were hauled out of the dock on a cradle because the width of paddle steamers had made existing dry docks useless. The steam engine was removed in the early 1960s. The ship is the PS *Dundee*, built at Renfrew in 1875 by W. Simons & Company. She worked the Tay Ferry service from 1875 until 1917 when she was sold to the Tay Steamboat Company for pleasure sailings. Later employed on the Queensferry passage on the Forth, she was scrapped in 1952.

HMS Unicorn was built for the Royal Navy in the Royal Dockyard at Chatham and launched in 1824. She was originally constructed as a two-decked 46-gun frigate built for war, but as Britain was now at peace following the Napoleonic War she was immediately 'housed fore and aft' by adding her distinctive roof, to preserve her for a potential future commission. This never came, and she spent her early life in reserve or 'ordinary', anchored on the River Medway until the 1850s. By the 1860s, with the rise of ironclad ships and steam propulsion, the ship's potential as a fighting frigate ended and between 1857 and 1862 she became a powder hulk for the Royal Arsenal at Woolwich. After another period laid up 'in ordinary' in 1873 she was towed to the Earl Grey Dock at Dundee in 1873 and the following year was refitted and commissioned as a Royal Naval Reserve Drill Ship. In 1906 she was lent to Clyde Division Royal Naval Volunteer Reserve and in 1926 was turned over to East Scottish Division RNVR. In 1962 she was moved to Camperdown Dock and then in 1963 to Victoria Dock. In 1969 the Ministry of Defence handed her over to the new Unicorn Preservation Society and in 1975 she was opened to the public 'as Scotland's oldest ship'.

The SS *Terra Nova* was built in 1884 by the Dundee Shipbuilders Company and was the last whaler to be constructed at the city. She worked in the seal fishery in the Labrador Sea until 1904 when the Admiralty sent her to Antarctica as part of a relief mission to rescue Captain Robert Falcon Scott and his crew from the icebound *Discovery*. In 1909 she was bought for Scott's British Antarctic Expedition of 1910 at a cost of £12,500 (£1.25 million in today's money), and was reinforced from bow to stern, the hull made thicker with 7 feet of oak to protect her against the Antarctic ice. After the expedition ended in tragedy in March 1912, the ship resumed work in the Newfoundland seal fishery. In 1918 she was charted to transport coal from the mines at North Sydney to Bell Island and in 1942 she was chartered to carry supplies to base stations in Greenland. On 1 September 1943 she sent an SOS reporting that she had sprung a bad leak off Greenland. The US coastguard cutter *Atak* reached the ship the following day, rescued all aboard and set the vessel alight. The burning hulk was sunk by the *Atak*'s gunfire the same day, but it took 23 rounds of three-inch gunfire to finish the job. The figurehead had been removed in 1913 and is now in the Museum of Wales. In 2012 the wreck was discovered on the seabed.

The Royal Research Ship *Discovery*, which was launched in 1901, was built in Dundee for the British Antarctic Expedition of that year and was the first vessel to be constructed specifically for scientific research. Nevertheless, with her design based on the Dundee whalers, she was the last traditional wooden three-masted ship to be built in the United Kingdom. Robert Falcon Scott was chosen to be the leader of the expedition, the main purpose of which was to make magnetic surveys and carry out meteorological, oceanographic, geological and biological research. The mission was successful and made a major contribution to the understanding of the Antarctic continent. Scott and his colleagues also covered over 950 miles on Antarctica, venturing further south than any men before them. Subsequently, after service as a merchant ship with the Hudson Bay Company before the First World War and taking munitions to Russia during it, the *Discovery* was taken into the service of the British Government in 1923, becoming the first Royal Research Ship. She made two further voyages to Antarctica, firstly in 1925 when the expedition's mission was to research whale stocks, the migration pattern of whales and to provide a scientific basis for regulation of the whaling industry. Then from 1929 to 1931, she served as the base for the British, Australian and New Zealand Antarctic Research Expedition, a major scientific and territorial quest in what is now the Australian Antarctic Territory. The brief this time was twofold: to chart the coastline, islands, rocks and shoals between Queen Mary Land and Enderby Island and 'to plant the British Flag wherever you find it practical to do so'. On her return she was moored in London as a static training ship and visitor centre until 1979. That year she was placed in the care of the Maritime Trust as a museum ship and in 1986 a new home was offered by Dundee Heritage Trust. On 3 April 1986 she berthed at Victoria Dock where she remains as the centrepiece of the Discovery Point Visitor Centre.

This 70-foot-high steam and hydraulic coal hoist was erected at the Stannergate on the Dundee waterfront in 1902. The principle of its operation was that railway wagons were to be brought into the coal hoist and raised up, then when they were at the right height the mechanism would tip them so that the coal fell out onto the sloping side. The sloping coal slide could be lowered down and angled to get the coal into the right part of the ship's hold, and the ship would be winched forward or astern by the ship's crew to further assist in the correct placing of the cargo. Its construction cost had originally been estimated in 1900 at £10,345 but another £4,500 had to be added the following year, when it was already being pilloried in the local newspapers as a unprofitable 'white elephant', pointing out that most coal hoisted on it was bunker coal and very little was for export. The hoist's final cost was £15,292 (around £1.8 million in today's money). At the time operations commenced there had been no foreseen difficulty with the Dundee & Arbroath Joint Line Railway Company working the spur line to the hoist, but the company hadn't been approached before the hoist was built so now it seized its opportunity not to comply until the Harbour Trustees gave them 4 or 5 acres of ground and disposed of other harbour property to them. The majority of the hoist's trustees would not be coerced by the railway company, declaring that they would rather the hoist stood idle for the next two years. This is exactly what happened and the dispute was not settled until September 1904, when a new goods and passenger station at Dundee East was promised to be built for the railway company. There were no coalfields in Forfarshire or Angus, so one of the aims behind the building of the hoist was to capitalise on the coal fields of Fife by making Dundee the loading port for ships transporting the coal elsewhere. But the city lost out to Methil, which became Scotland's premier coal port, moving three million tons of coal annually at its peak. The coal hoist fell out of use; the jetty was sold to the Caledon Shipbuilding and Engineering Company Ltd in 1918 and the hoist was dismantled to make way for the new Caledon Yard.

The remains of a large humpback whale that swam into the Firth of Tay in December 1883. This caused great excitement locally and the whale was harpooned in a hunt on 31 December. It escaped but was found floating dead off Stonehaven a week later. Christened 'The Great Tay Whale' and 'The Monster', it was bought for £226 by John Woods, a local entrepreneur, and towed into Dundee where it is pictured here exhibited in his yard after dissection. Its size was 40 feet long with flukes measuring 11 feet 4 inches. On the first Sunday it was exhibited in the yard 12,000 people paid to see it. The Regius Professor of Anatomy at Aberdeen University, Sir John Struthers, dissected the whale, much of the time in public with a military band playing in the background, all organised by Woods. Even the doggerel poet, the great McGonagall, couldn't resist writing a notoriously bad poem on 'The Famous Tay Whale'. The skeleton was removed before Woods had the flesh embalmed; the carcass was then stuffed and sewn up to be taken on a profitable tour around Britain. The skeleton is now on display at the McManus Galleries in Dundee.

In 1908 the Admiralty began looking for a place on the east coast of Scotland to build a submarine base, finally settling on Dundee. They took a five year lease from 1 September 1909 and on 27 November that year the 7th Submarine Flotilla left Portsmouth and arrived at Dundee on the 29th, entering their base in King William IV Dock the next day. This lease was extended many times and finally expired on 30 September 1920.

Two submarines approaching the base. The nearest is B-Class No. 24 and the further one is C-Class No. 51. Below, the submarines are nearing the quayside. The ghostly outline of the Tay Rail Bridge features in the background of both pictures.

Those same two submarines of the 7th Flotilla arriving at Dundee from exercises, with one of the Tay dredgers in the background. When war broke out in 1939 a depot ship and six submarines were on a courtesy visit to the Tay and began their war duty from Dundee. One of these, the *Oxley*, was the first British submarine to be lost in the North Sea, a victim of friendly fire. By 1945 Dundee had become a significant submarine base and, besides those of the Royal Navy, hosted submarines from Poland, the Free French, the Netherlands, Russia and Norway. Both the 2nd and 9th Submarine Flotillas were stationed at Dundee between 1939 and 1945.

HMS Vulcan, on the left of the picture below, was launched in 1889 as a torpedo boat depot ship. She was later converted to a submarine tender in 1908-09 and is seen here off Dundee in 1908, having been brought from the Nore (an area of the Thames near Sheerness) to serve as a dormitory for the submarine crews. At the outbreak of war in 1914 the *Vulcan* and the 7th Flotilla were transferred to war stations at Rosyth. Later, she was renamed *HMS Defiance III* in 1931 and used for training at Torpoint in Cornwall. She was scrapped in 1955.

W.B. Thompson founded the Tay Foundry in 1866 and W.B. Shipbuilding in 1869. He opened the shipyard in 1874 and in 1896 restructured the shipbuilding company as the Caledon Shipbuilding & Engineering Company Limited. The shipyard traded for more than a century and built more than 500 ships. In 1968 Caledon merged with Henry Robb of Leith to form Robb Caledon Shipbuilding Limited. Industrial relations were not good; a series of strikes during the middle of the twentieth century bedevilled the Caledon yard and it built its last ship in 1980. The yard closed to shipbuilding in 1981 and nowadays repairs North Sea oil rigs.

Dundee's first public swimming pool was situated at the Earl Grey Dock and opened in 1848. Built as the Olympia Stadium but known locally as the 'Shorers', it had three main salt water pools and Turkish baths, plunge baths, foam baths and aeratone baths. It also had a café. It introduced changing boxes and diving stages in the 1870s and in the 1880s advertised a 'Skilled shampooer in attendance'. The baths were enlarged in 1873 and reconstructed again in 1909/10, when a viewing gallery was added, as seen in this picture. Ladies also got their own pool. Mixed bathing was allowed from 1923 but only on Thursday afternoons, although this was extended over time. The baths were demolished in 1974 and replaced by new baths built on an adjacent site; in turn these were replaced in 2013 by baths in the New Olympia Leisure Centre.

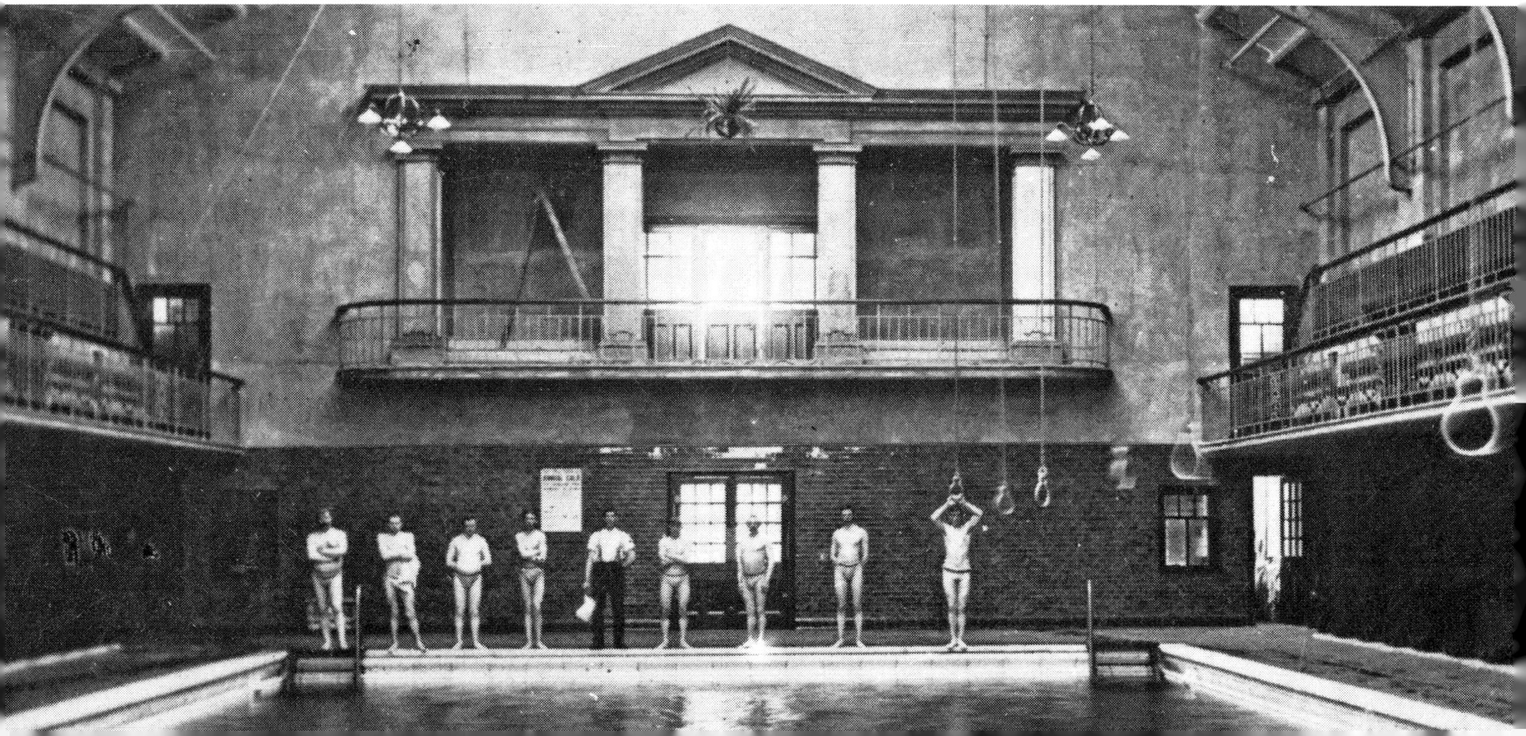

The river is behind the photographer in this view looking northwards from the Esplanade in Edwardian days. The hipped roof of the building below street level belongs to the North British Railway's Tay Bridge Station. The buildings behind it at street level are various good sheds belonging to the rival Caledonian Railway, whose West Station lies just beyond them, crowned by its magnificent clock tower. A line of horse-drawn cabs is waiting on the corner. The station was designed in 1889 by Thomas Barr, the Caledonian Railway's chief engineer, and was built of red sandstone in a Scots Baronial style. The station closed on 3 May 1965 and was demolished; no trace of it remains today. Opposite the station is the tall domed building at the junction of Union Street and Whitehall Crescent that opened in 1899 as Mather's Temperance Hotel but is now the Malmaison Hotel. The

carter in the foreground is giving his horse some refreshment out of a bucket and his cart is inscribed 'Midland Railway', which is odd as this railway's tracks reached no further north than Carlisle. The ornate drinking fountain on the right was designed by city architect James Thomson and donated to the city in 1908 by Lord Provost William Longair to commemorate visits to the city by Queen Alexandra. She paid the city several brief visits during the first decade of the twentieth century when she alighted at Dundee while travelling by sea to Denmark to visit her family. The fountain has since been removed to Discovery Point but has lost the cross and ball from the top of the crown.

Magdalen Green lies at the west end of the waterfront and extends to more than 20 acres. Nowadays owned by Dundee City Council, it is the city's oldest park and its name is said to derive from a chapel, or possibly a nunnery, that once stood in the vicinity of the present-day Step Row. It once extended right down to the river before the road and railway intervened. In the nineteenth century the Green was the site of a number of large political meetings in the cause of electoral reform. Its fine Victorian bandstand was built in 1890 at the Saracen Foundry of Walter Macfarlane & Co. of Glasgow; it was restored in 1991 and repaired again in 2009. The factory seen here is the Seafield Works of Thomson, Shepherd & Co. (Sanderson Carpets), a five-storey spinning mill and jute carpet factory dating from 1861. It closed in 1986 and was converted into residential housing. The railway lines are those of the Caledonian Railway running from Dundee West Station to Perth and Glasgow, while the sidings in the foreground are those of the North British Railway.

This public bowling green was one of eight new greens commissioned by the city council in 1908 as part of schemes to help relieve unemployment in the city. It was opened on 20 September 1909, at a cost of £389 (around £38,000 in today's money), and was situated on the Magdalen Green just to the west of Riverside Approach and close to the railway line to Perth and Glasgow. This photograph dates from *c.* 1914. The bowling green has long since gone but it's faint outline can still be seen from the air.

Independent of the Army, volunteer battalions were created in the 1850s. The 1st Forfar (Dundee) Rifle Volunteer Corps was formed in 1859 and the 3rd Forfar (Dundee Highland) Rifle Volunteer Corps a year later. The 1st Forfarshire consisted of about 800 men and the 3rd Forfarshire consisted about 600. In 1881, due to army reforms, they became part of the Black Watch and were later integrated into the Territorial Army. They served in both world wars, fighting many of the major battles on the Western Front during the First World War, while in the Second they saw action in the Battle of France, in North Africa and Sicily, and in Europe from D-Day. They continued in the post-war army until 1975. The principal building in Magdalen Yard Road in the background was Dundee's Institution for the Blind, which became Royal in 1915. The wording on the roof says 'Institution for the Blind'. In 1997, the building was converted into ten sheltered flats for elderly people and is now called Servite Court.

Bellefield Avenue is lined with dignified four-storey tenements built in the early 1890s and leads northwards from Magdelene Yard Road up to Seafield Road. This view is from the bottom end of the road; the garden walls are nowadays devoid of their ornate cast-iron railings which were no doubt ripped out during the Second World War to make armaments. Two lines of parked cars have nowadays replaced the delivery carts and the people in this Edwardian picture, while the present-day view

beyond the top of the road is of the modern houses in Seafield Road and Seafield Close, which has replaced this dismal view of the chimneys of the Tayfield jute works. These were the works of Hugh and Alexander Scott who went into business in 1857. Their firm manufactured jute as well as other textile products and eventually moved into polypropylene manufacture. It was taken over by Amoco UK Ltd in 1985.

Dundee Tay Bridge Station was built in 1878 by the North British Railway as part of the Tay Rail Bridge project and was one of three stations in the city, along with the Caledonian Railway's West Station and the Dundee & Arbroath Joint Railway's East Station. The latter two closed in 1965 and 1959 respectively, and Tay Bridge remains the city's only station. It is an island platform station with two bays at the west end and is located in a deep, dressed-stone cutting. The brick-built station building is two storeys high with the glazed hipped roof of the second floor at ground level. As part of the redevelopment of Dundee City Centre in the 1960s the original public entrance of the station was demolished to accommodate the new Tay Road Bridge offramps, with a new smaller structure replacing it. However, a £38 million station incorporating a ticket hall and hotel was built in 2018 to replace the old surface buildings as part of the Dundee Waterfront Regeneration Project. The station connects the west and east sides of the city with a passenger-carrying through line. To the east of the station is Dock Street Tunnel and beyond it the line emerges alongside the former Dundee East Station at Camperdown Junction. This picture shows a quiet afternoon looking eastwards along Platform 4 in the mid 1960s. The Refreshment Rooms – now part of the Pumpkin Cafe – have a grisly history, for they were used in the identification of the bodies of victims of the Tay Bridge Disaster. The passengers sitting on the platform seat would have been waiting for a train to take them further up the east coast to Arbroath, Montrose or Aberdeen.

Opposite page: At Dundee Tay Bridge Station in July 1956, locomotive No. 67502 simmers Platform 4. This was the last of the 21 locomotives of Class C16 that were designed in 1915 by the North British Railway's Locomotive Superintendent, William Paton Reid. This was a batch of 'Atlantic' type superheated locomotives with side tanks and a 4-4-2 wheel arrangement (four leading wheels, four driving wheels and two trailing wheels). This particular locomotive was built at the North British Locomotive Company's works in Glasgow and launched into service on the North British Railway on 31 March 1921. It was withdrawn from service on 30 April 1960 and scrapped at British Railways' Inverurie Works two months later.

A Diesel Multiple Unit (DMU), built for British Railways by the Metro-Cammell company, at rest at Platform 2, Tay Bridge Station, in the late 1960s. It would have arrived on a stopping service from either Glasgow, Edinburgh or Perth.

A view from the west end of Tay Bridge Station, looking over intricate pointwork towards the West Signal Box. Tay Bridge Station had signal boxes at either end but both boxes closed in 1985, being replaced by the Dundee Signalling Centre. In this late 1960s picture an express for the south, heading to Edinburgh, Glasgow or perhaps even London Kings Cross, is leaving Platform 1 and beginning the climb to Tay Rail Bridge. The Mk 1 First Class carriage is wearing the newly-introduced colours of Pearl Grey upper panels and Rail Blue lower panels, separated by a ribbon of white.

Dundee East Station was the terminus of the Dundee & Arbroath Joint Railway. It opened in 1857 and was reconstructed in 1893. Known to Dundonians as the 'Black Hole', the station had a trainshed with a fanlight at its west end, as seen in this 1955 photograph. There were two platforms under the roof and two more platforms outside, one on either side. The station became redundant as local lines closed and longer-distance services transferred to Tay Bridge Station. It closed in 1959 and left to crumble before demolition in 1964. Nothing remains of it today apart from a few sidings.

Ex-North British Railway 4-4-2T No. 67490 standing at a deserted platform at Dundee East Station, flanked by rakes of ex-London & North Eastern Railway (LNER) non-corridor coaches. This class of locomotive was another designed in 1915 by William Paton Reid. It would probably have previously brought a passenger train from Arbroath into the station, which would have formed the outgoing local train service seen in the next picture.

This stopping passenger train at Dundee East Station is probably bound for Arbroath, and is headed by Class J39 0-6-0-type tender engine No. 64792. This class of locomotive was designed in 1926 by Nigel (later Sir Nigel) Gresley, Chief Mechanical Engineer of the London & North Eastern Railway).

Dundee West Station was designed in 1889 by Thomas Barr, the Caledonian Railway's chief engineer, and was built of red sandstone in Scots Baronial style. An earlier station, made of wood and with two platforms, had been opened by the Dundee & Perth Railway in 1847. After the Dundee & Perth merged with the Scottish Central Railway in 1863, an improved station was opened in 1866. This only lasted for 23 years before it too was deemed too small and demolished to make way for the building in the picture. A large carriage turning area was created in front of the new station which had four terminal platforms with a glazed trainshed roof 500 feet long and 112 feet wide. Trains ran to Glasgow and the south while local traffic took passengers to such places as Perth, Gleneagles, Crieff, Blairgowrie and Newtyle. It closed on 1 May 1965 and was demolished to make way for a link road to the new Tay Road Bridge, a car park and several new buildings. Author John Minnis has described the demolition of this wonderful station as 'perhaps the most tragic loss of a piece of railway architecture in Scotland'.

Dundee West Motive Power Depot (MPD) in 1954, with several locomotives just visible inside the shed. The small tank engine is one of many 'Class 782' 0-6-0T locomotives designed for the Caledonian Railway in 1896 by their Locomotive Superintendent, John Farquharson McIntosh. The large locomotive on the left is one of the 'Class WD' or 'Austerity' 2-8-0 locomotives built for the Ministry of Supply in 1943; these were based on Sir William Stanier's 1935-built 2-8-0 locomotives for the London Midland and Scottish Railway, but with no refinements whatsoever, cost reduction being the priority. A total of 935 of these locomotives were made, the order split between the North British Locomotive Company in Glasgow (545) and Vulcan Foundry of Newton-le-Willows, Lancashire (390). All but three saw service in mainland Europe after D-Day. After the war, 733 became part of British Railways in 1948. They were used on heavy freight trains in many parts of the country, and although scrapping began in the early 1960s the survivors lasted until the end of steam on British Railways in 1968. Dundee West MPD itself had been built by the Caledonian Railway in 1885 and was in use until the mid 1980s. The site has been redeveloped with a car park and children's playground.

John Smith was in business as a wholesale fruit merchant with premises at 43 and 45 Yeaman Shore alongside Dundee West Station. In 1927 he moved from Yeaman Shore to more commodious premises at 31 Crichton Street.

Crichton Street comes in from the left of the picture at the side of the Caird Hall. The bus stance in the centre is now the Shore Terrace car park; the facing building fronting onto Castle Street was formerly the Assembly Rooms but is now The Wine Press bar.

This was the Dock Street bus stance at the back of the Caird Hall, nowadays the Shore Terrace car park. This decrepit single-decker Daimler bus was built in 1938 as Number 91, renumbered 31 in 1950 and was withdrawn from service in 1958.

Three double-deckers at the Dock Street stance. The nearest bus, No.113, is a Daimler dating from 1936. It was withdrawn from service in 1953 and became a driver trainer and tree lopper. In 1966 it was sold to a vehicle dealer in Pittenweem. The bus in the middle, No. 125, which is entering the bus stance, is also a Daimler but of 1950 vintage. It was withdrawn from service in 1970 and subsequently used by Dundee Corporation Building Department. The third bus, on the left of the lamp standard, is an unidentified AEC.

This building, in the angle between Dock Street and Exchange Street, was designed in 1828 by George Smith of Edinburgh as Dundee's Coffee House, Assembly Rooms, Merchants' Library and Reading Room. In a significant change of use it reopened as the Alhambra Music Hall in 1866. There were 3,416 visitors on the opening night which was beset with delays because of the non-arrival of several artistes engaged to appear. This may have caused disturbances in the audience because the following week's programme warned that police would be in attendance! In a further change of use the building reopened as the City Assembly Halls in 1889 and was henceforth to be used for balls and 'high class' concerts. This, too, only lasted for about twenty years. In 1911 it became the City Masonic Temple. The Masons vacated the hall in 1924 and the building became the printing works of David Winter & Son until 1993, when they relocated to the Dunsinane Industrial Estate. It is now the premises of The Wine Press bar.

The Dundee Sailors' Home was a lodging house which up to 80 sailors could use while waiting for their next passage. It cost over £11,000, plus £1,000 for furnishings. The five-storey L-shaped building on the corner of Dock Street and Candle Lane was very spacious, and facilities included a chapel and dining, reading, recreation and smoking rooms. High up on its exterior are carved the names of British naval heroes: Nelson, Cook, Blake, Wood, Duncan and Napier. It was opened in 1881 and later, because of falling numbers of seamen using it, it also opened to the general public as a hostel in 1930. It closed as a sailors' home and hostel in 1987. It stood empty for many years and conversion into twelve flats was carried out in 2007.

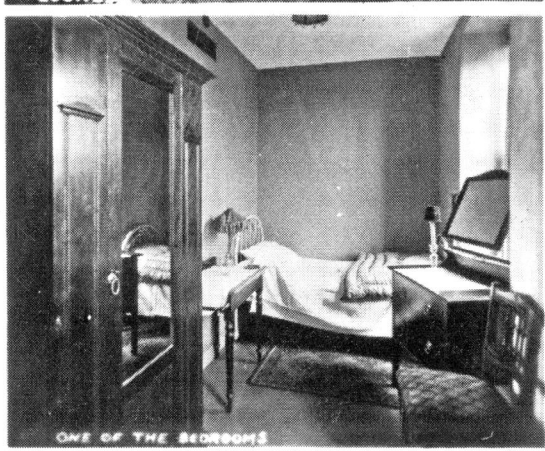

A postcard showing some of the facilities at the Sailors' Home, which must have seemed like heaven to men returning from a long voyage.

DUNDEE SAILORS' HOME AND HOSTEL.

This very substantial building, erected at a cost of about £12,000 was opened in 1881. Facing south, it has a commanding view of the Silvery Tay and the hills of Fife. It was originally built for whalers and seamen using the port of Dundee, but since the Great War the number of seamen using the Home has dropped off considerably.

A Hostel has been added to the Home and is now being managed as a Hotel or Y.M. Hostel, catering for Commercial Travellers, Chauffeurs, Transport Drivers, Soldiers, Cyclists and Holiday-makers. The Hostel is just five minutes from Tay Ferries, Railway and Bus Stations. A 2d bus run takes you to Dundee Corporation's two golf courses and its various tennis courts and public parks. The principal Cinemas are within ten minutes' walk of the Hostel.

Dundee is favourably situated as a centre for tourists, and offers splendid opportunities for exploring Scotland with all its scenic beauty and rugged Highland grandeur. The Home is within easy reach of Albert Square from which half-day, day and long-distance coach tours start off during the summer season. The Carse of Gowrie, the Sidlaws, Glenisla, Glenshee, Glamis, Glen Clova and Glen Esk are all within a few hours of the city. Strathtay, Royal Deeside, the Perthshire Highlands, Inverness, Oban and Loch Lomond district are popular objectives on day tours.

During the summer also the Railway Companies—both the L.M.S. and the L.N.E.R. serve Dundee—offer some delightful day and evening trips at exceedingly reduced rates.

DUNDEE SAILORS' HOME AND HOSTEL.
'Phone 6478. 'Grams: Sailors' Home, Dundee.

TARIFF.
"A" FLAT
(Officers, Commercial Travellers, Holiday-makers etc.)

Single Bedrooms	2/- & 3/-
Room and Breakfast	4/- & 5/6
Luncheons	1/6 & 2/-
High Teas	1/6 & 2/-
Board and Lodgings per day	6/- & 8/-

Reduced Terms for Periods.

"B" and "C" FLAT
(Sailors, Soldiers, Chauffeurs, Cyclists, etc.)

Room and Breakfast	3/-
Single Bedroom	1/6
Luncheons	1/6
High Teas	1/6
Board and Lodgings per day	5/-

Reduced Terms for Periods.

There are 34 Single Bedrooms and 11 Double Bedrooms (2 beds), 8 Bathrooms, H. & C. Water and Electric Light. Large Dining Room, Spacious Smoking and Reading Room, Comfortable Lounge.

RICHARD O. S. LINN, Superintendent.

A tariff card for the Sailors' Home c. 1930, after it had become a hostel.

Fish Street on the right of the picture ran from the foot of Crichton Street to the foot of Union Street and at one time its mid-eighteenth century houses were the residences of some of the city's leading merchants. The centre building probably dates from 1591 and is believed to have been built by Provost John Pierson. In the eighteenth century it was a custom house and was later known as 'Drummond Castle', this name apparently originating from a novel in which it appears as a castle of the fictional Drummond family. This view is from the Greenmarket, *c.* 1880. This area was demolished as part of the improvement scheme which saw the building of Whitehall Street and Whitehall Crescent. However, the site of this building wasn't developed until the 1970s when an office block was built on it.

Yeaman Shore, seen from Dundee West Station and showing the rear of Reid's Waverley Temperance Hotel and Restaurant at 7 Union Street. This hotel was demolished in 1899 and replaced by Mather's Temperance Hotel, nowadays the Malmaison Hotel. Yeaman Shore was named after the Yeaman family who had a property here; George Yeaman was twice Provost in the early 1700s.

Only part of the tower of the Caledonian Railway's West Station is visible in this 1912 photograph taken from South Union Street, the station itself being hidden by that railway's goods offices. Union Street extends up the centre, with Whitehall Crescent curving around the far side of Mather's Hotel on the right-hand corner. The roadsweeper is busy with his brush and shovel. When the city's Police Commissioners were first appointed in 1824, they were responsible for lighting, paving and cleansing the town as well as policing it; their sanitary department employed about 124 carters and scavengers who collected horse droppings daily. These were sold to the farmers of the surrounding districts.

Margaret Mathers first opened a temperance hotel in 1860. Her temperance business flourished and she opened Mathers' Temperance Hotel in 1900 at the junction of Union Street and Whitehall Crescent. It was a powerful symbol of the prohibition movement and became one of the foremost commercial hotels in Scotland. In 1969 it was sold and renamed the Tay Centre Hotel. It later became the Tay Hotel and then fell into disrepair before being bought by the Malmaison chain who reopened it in 2014 as the Malmaison Dundee. The church visible at the far end of Union Street is the Parish Church of St Mary.

A view looking towards Whitehall Street from the other end of Whitehall Crescent and it has barely changed today. The large department store of Thomas Justice & Sons Limited's on the corner of Whitehall Street, while the premises on the nearside of Whitehall Street are Cooper & Company, the Whitehall Restaurant, and Christie's Temperance Hotel with McKay Bros & Co. occupying its ground floor. Across the road is Talbert Thomson's tobacconist's shop, the Whitehall Crescent Post Office and Ross Callaghan & Co.'s cutlers shop.

A corner of the Greenmarket on a market day. North of Earl Grey Dock and south of the High Street, this was Dundee's foremost marketplace and venue for fairs. The building on the right was the old custom house seen on p. 36. The buildings in the centre were demolished to build part of the north side of Whitehall Crescent (seen on the left) while the remainder of the Greenmarket buildings were demolished to make way for the Caird Hall.

This is an 1880s photograph of Castle Lane which was located at the foot of Crichton Street and on the east side of the Greenmarket. Castle Court is the tall building at the end of the lane, with a passage running through to the court itself and on to Castle Street. The residents of the court belonged to the shore folk of Dundee whalers and fishers, who lived in a distinct community of clanned families. In January 1915 the Town Council purchased Castle Court for £55 for the city improvement scheme and its site is now covered by the Caird Hall and City Square.

The part of Dundee called The Vault lay to the south of the High Street, behind the Town House, where it met St Clement's Lane; it took its name from the vaulted pend or archway at its foot. It was predominantly a residential area but there were a considerable number of public houses and other places for social activity such as coffee houses and it was well-used by merchants arriving at Dundee by sea. This picture doesn't do it full justice; it was the second most important location in the burgh after the Market Place for commercial dealings, and the area was demolished in 1930 when City Square was built.

Reform Street, named after the 1832 Reform Act, runs in this picture from the High Street, up past the Howff graveyard and ends at the High School in Meadowside. The street frontage was designed by George Angus of Edinburgh who had already designed the High School and the Dundee Sheriff and Justice of the Peace Courts. The street was opened in 1833 but the last building, Lamb's Hotel on the corner of Meadowside, wasn't completed until 1867. The street was the first Dundee thoroughfare conceived as a unit of architectural composition. Among merchants who moved their businesses to the new street were two shoemakers, one hatter, five clothiers and two silk merchants. By 1864 the street hosted a dozen tailors alone and became Scotland's Savile Row. The pillared building in the distance is Dundee High School which is built in the Doric style of architecture.

The Royal British Hotel at the corner of High Street and Castle Street dates from 1842. In 1965 it became the Dundee University Hall of Residence, named after James Chalmers (1782-1853) who was the inventor of the adhesive postage stamp and whose shop was once nearby at 10 Castle Street. The Hall of Residence has now closed and the building is unoccupied apart from the ground floor which is taken by a Braithwaite's tea and coffee shop (established in 1868 and on this site since 1932) and two other businesses.

Seagate was for many years the town's main street. It runs eastwards from the High Street to Blackscroft, which then continues eastwards into Broughty Ferry Road. This photograph of the head of Seagate was taken in 1876 from St Paul's Episcopal Church (later Cathedral) at the Burnhead. All the buildings were demolished in the late-nineteenth century with the creation of Commercial Street.

The picture is taken from Barrack Street, looking up Constitution Road towards Dundee Law. The two-storey building on the right of the picture, which was built in 1845-46 by Thomas Cuthbert as coachbuilding premises, was demolished in the late nineteenth century to build the new Post Office in a French Renaissance style in 1895-98, and this building still stands, although empty as the Post Office has since migrated to Whitehall Street. The building on the immediate left was the Central Reading Rooms, now part of the Dundee Art Gallery and Museums Collections Unit. The three-storey building beyond it, across the road, is still recognisable today and its ground floor is nowadays used for entertainment by the Number 1 Bar. Further up Constitution Road the buildings with the elaborate chimneys on the right side of the street are still standing but everything beyond them has been swept away to build the University of Abertay Dundee. The buildings on the left side of the street have been more fortunate. These include the 1839 Watt Institute, now the premises of Dundee Voluntary Action Ltd.

This 1971 picture, with the old Public Baths and Wash House in Constable Street in the background, shows the site of old worksheds that were uncovered during demolition of tenements in Blackscroft. The sheds were probably used between 1790 and 1830 for fish smoking and making tallow from whales. The arches in the background were built to take the burn that flowed under Constable Street down to the Tay.

The Trades Hall opened in 1776. It stood at the east end of the High Street for a century and was home to the Nine Incorporated Trades of Dundee, each of which was given its own room in the building in which to conduct business. The hall also acted as a theatre and the Dundee Exchange Coffee Rooms and newspaper room and had a bank from 1833. It was doomed by the 1871 City Improvement Act which, by widening the narrow Seagate and Murraygate, squeezed it into oblivion. The building was demolished in 1878 and the bell from the cupola was kept and put in the spire of the Town House.

Dating from 1785 and originally known as the English Chapel, this building at the west end of the High Steet faced the Trades Hall across the Market Place. It became known as the Union Hall after the departure of its episcopal congregation once St Paul's Church (later cathedral) had been built. This photograph dates from 1876, shortly before the Hall's demolition, but its former location can be determined with reference to the surviving building on the left. The twin-roofed building on the right is Our Lady Warkstairs, built in the early sixteenth century and, by the time of its demolition in 1876, was the last of the old timber-fronted houses in Dundee.

The east end of the High Street around 1908, with Murraygate to the left of the Clydesdale Bank and the beginning of Seagate just visible on the right between the buildings. The bank, which was designed by William Spence and replaced the Trades Hall in 1878, dominates the picture in the centre. The open-top tram (No. 18) passing H. Samuel's jewellers shop at the end of the High Street is heading for Baxter Park. It is one of the first two batches of open-top trams that were introduced in 1900 and 1902. On the right a man is unloading goods from the cart while the carter appears to be holding the horse steady; behind them another open-top tram is heading down Seagate.

Whitehall Street was built under the 1858 improvement plan and opened in 1883. Later, Alexander Ewing & Co. Ltd, drapers, was established in the prime location of Whitehall House on the corner of Whitehall Street and Nethergate. In the 1940s it was taken over by House of Fraser though it now stands empty.

William Pringle Laird was a seedsman, bulb importer, florist and nursery proprietor. By 1845 his business premises were in Nethergate and the firm later moved to High Street premises next to the Town House as seen here. Both buildings were demolished as part of the construction of the City Square and in March 1935 Laird & Sinclair moved to Crichton Street, overlooking the new square. The company operated until at least 1971.

In this picture from around 1940, W. P. Laird & Sinclair's new shop is on the corner of Crichton Street at its junction with the west end of the High Street. The building with the tower is the Parish Church of St Mary's in Nethergate. Known as the Old Steeple, this building – 156 feet tall – was completed in the late fifteenth century (the church itself was founded in 1190). It is Dundee's oldest building.

A busy scene at the west end of the High Street with Overgate on the right and Nethergate on the left. The tram in the middle is one of a batch built specially for the Lochee service in 1930, while the other two were allocated to the Blackness to Downfield service and were originally open-top and unvestibuled. The spire in the distance belongs to St Paul's Meadowside Church of Scotland. The building in the centre of the picture with Lipton's shop was known as General Monck's lodging because he stayed in it after capturing the city in 1651. The house dated from the 1400s and once had a row of arches on the ground floor which housed shops set back from the street. These were known as luckens and earned the building the name of the Luckenbooth. This small area of property was known as 'The Island' and all the buildings were demolished in 1964 to make way for the second phase of the Overgate Centre.

Another photograph of the buildings on 'The Island'. The date cannot be later than 1956 because there is a tram in the picture. Strathtay House on the corner of Reform Street is not only recognisable today but is still occupied by Boots the Chemists. The buildings in the High Street on the nearside of Reform Street have also survived and, now refurbished, form an attractive north side of the High Street.

This photograph shows the north side of the High Street at its junction with Reform Street. The photograph must have been taken before June 1910 because that was when H. Samuel moved into the facing corner building and H. & W. Tulloch moved next door into 3 Reform Street. Samuel's now occupy the corner building and most of the former McGillivray shop next door as well. The Boots shop is on the opposite corner of Reform Street in the former Strathtay House. The Central Billiard Rooms in the picture are now the Dundee Backpackers Hostel, fronted by three retail shops.

A 1950s view from the very eastern end of Nethergate, looking along High Street towards the Clydesdale Bank at its far end. Tram No. 28, probably bound for Maryfield but with Lochee already indicated for its return journey, was the last tram to be bought by Dundee Corporation Tramways. This batch of ten trams was built by Brush Traction of Loughborough in 1930 and they differed from the other Dundee trams by having a wide body specially for the Lochee route.

This photograph was taken at almost the same location and date as the picture above. The lady on the left is running to catch the 1902-vintage Tram No. 48 which already looks fairly crowded as it heads for Maryfield.

Tram No. 28 again, this time going along a very busy Reform Street towards the High Street. It's obvious from this picture why trams were such a hindrance to other traffic.

Murraygate is one of the oldest streets in Dundee and legend has it that it was named after Thomas Randolph, 1st Earl of Moray, who fought alongside Robert the Bruce at the Battle of Bannockburn in 1314. It connects the east end of the High Street with Cowgate, and this picture is a view from the High Street up to the top of Murraygate. Commercial Street, from where the oncoming tram has turned, is on the left. The department store on the left is that of D. M. Brown which employed more than 400 people. The store became known as 'D.M.'s' to generations of shoppers even after it was acquired in 1952 by House of Fraser. The name D. M. Brown continued to be used until 1972 when it was changed to Arnott's. The store closed in 2002 and it was divided into seven retail units but retained the original 1870s façade and dome as well as various major internal features.

The Maypole Dairy Company was an early chain of British dairies which rose to become the biggest in the country. It was the first dairy company to promote the widespread use of margarine as an alternative to butter and it also sold staples such as eggs, tea and condensed milk. The company was a high-volume, low-margin business and focused on working class areas. It peaked in 1928 when it had 1,040 stores and eighteen creameries. The brand survived until 1964 when it was absorbed by Allied Suppliers, and the final Maypole Dairy closed in 1970. This shop at 92/93 High Street, seen here in 1905, boasted an elaborate façade and a shop window heavily promoting the company's margarine. The shop was located on the corner of D. M. Brown's store but when the latter wanted the premises for its own expansion Maypole moved in 1908 down the street to No. 64 High Street.

This 1940 picture shows Murraygate at its junction with Commercial Street. The whole area is nowadays pedestrianised but tram tracks have been left down for old times' sake. The tower of St Andrew's Parish Church can be seen in the distance, rising above nearer buildings, but the building in Cowgate displaying a large advertisement for Wills's Capstan Cigarettes was demolished and replaced (together with other buildings in Cowgate and Panmure Street) by the modern Wellgate Shopping Centre which was opened in 1978. The La Scala cinema (opened 1913, closed 1965, demolished 2008) is further down the street on the left-hand side of Murraygate. The department store of G. L. Wilson on the corner with Commercial Street was founded in 1894 and popularly known as 'The Corner'. The business closed in 1971 and the building was redeveloped in the 1990s but happily the exterior was refurbished to its original state. Smith Brothers on the opposite side of Murraygate was founded around 1886 and was in the business of furriers, clothiers and house furnishers.

Another view of Murraygate. Gavin Laurie Wilson operated a warehouse in Cupar, Fife, before opening this store in 1894. Approaching down Murraygate, Tram No. 44 is about to enter the High Street on its way to West Park, on the Perth Road. This tram was built open-top in 1902 but by the time of this picture the top deck had been enclosed for many years.

This shop at 66 Murraygate is listed in the Dundee 1906/07 Directory as belonging to James Nelson & Sons Ltd, butchers. The displayed prices are eyewatering – cuts of meat at 6d and 8d (2.5p and 3.3p) while the most expensive of the very large joints hanging from the rail costs 5/- (25p)! The building is nowadays occupied by a different business and the façade has been altered unrecognisably.

Pictured in 1950, Tram No. 43, of 1902 vintage and originally built with an open top deck, is passing the Gaumont Cinema (on the right of the picture) in Cowgate and taking the curve round into Murraygate on its way to Ninewells. The Gaumont would later go on to become the Odeon and, later still, the Deja Vu nightclub.

This 1910 picture looks along Cowgate from the end of Panmure Street, with Murraygate running off to the right between the tall buildings on the corner. The shops in the picture were erected in 1908-09 when Cowgate was widened and their appearance is almost identical today. The last building in the row is the King's Theatre which was opened in 1909.

The Gaumont cinema on Cowgate was originally the King's Theatre and Hippodrome which opened in 1909. It held 2,500 people and had a lavish interior. It became King's Theatre Cinema in 1928 and was the Gaumont from 1950 to 1973. From 1973 to 1981 it was the Odeon and then a bingo hall until 1994. In 2000 it became the Déjà Vu Nightclub but this closed in 2016 and the empty building has been on the Buildings at Risk Register ever since.

The land of this burial ground in Meadowside used to be part of the gardens of Greyfriars Franciscan monastery, Greyfriars. In 1547 the monastery buildings were laid to ruin by an English army, sent by King Henry VIII's during his 'Rough Wooing' campaign, and its lands were confiscated during the Scottish Reformation of 1559/60. However, in 1564 Mary, Queen of Scots granted the land to the burgh of Dundee for use as a burial ground. It was also used for meetings of the Dundee Incorporated Trades. The land became known as The Howff, from the old Scottish word *howff*, meaning an enclosed open space. The last burial was in 1878 and it has one of the most important collections of tombstones in Scotland. The Renaissance-style building on the right of the picture is Friarfield House; it stands in Barrack Street and was opened in 1873 as the offices of Don Brothers, Buist & Co. Ltd, flax and jute spinners and manufacturers. Part of their massive Ward Mill with its ornate tower stands to its left; this building was demolished in 1964 but the offices have survived today as the premises of Dundee's Community Justice Services.

THE CENTRAL READING ROOM, DUNDEE.

The site of the Central Branch Library and Central Reading Room on the corner of Ward Road and Barrack Road was funded by £5,000 from Sir William Ogilvy Dalgleish, chairman of Baxter Brothers and a generous benefactor to many of Dundee's institutions. The building was paid for by Andrew Carnegie who opened the library himself on 12 September 1911. In 1901 he had gifted £37,000 for the formation of five branch libraries in Dundee, the other four being Arthurstone Terrace, Coldstone, Blackness, and St Roque's. The library was replaced by the Central Library in the Wellgate Centre in 1979 and the building is now the Collections Department of the McManus Art Gallery and Museum. Friarfield House is on the left of this picture.

This building in Ward Road dates from 1855 and was built as a Girls' Industrial School. If a girl was sent here it was more or less a punishment for her misdemeanours. In 1896 the school moved to a larger building on Blackness Road and the Salvation Army took over their former building. It now became a hostel that gave accommodation to the women who dominated the city's jute workforce. The sign above its gates reads 'The Salvation Army Working Women's Hotel'. It is nowadays their Strathmore Lodge Lifehouse, which comprises 25 flats and is equipped with reception, lounges, dining room, kitchen, laundry, pool room and gym.

Dundee's Girls' High School was built across Euclid Crescent in two stages between 1886 and 1890. It adjoined the Boys' High School building of 1832-34 and both school buildings are now the High School of Dundee.

Opposite page (upper): The Old Post Office was opened on 23 May 1862, though it was demolished as early as 1899. The city's post office had previously been based in many locations, ending up in premises under the Town House before this post office, seen here in 1878, was built. The road running across the picture is Ward Road (now Meadowside) and the one running between the buildings is Constitution Road. The ornamental fountain was later destroyed by a falling tree. The building on the left of the picture looks identical today and is the premises of Be Uniforms, while the offices of publishers D. C. Thomson & Co Ltd are on the site of the post office and lie facing the Albert Institute (now the McManus Galleries).

Below: Courier Building, the headquarters of publishers D.C. Thomson Limited, stands on the site of the Old Post Office of 1862 and, in this view, the front of the building is facing Albert Square with the portico of the High School on the right and Ward Road (now Meadowside) entering the picture from the left. Founded by David Couper Thomson in 1905, the firm is best known for publishing the *Dundee Courier*, the *Evening Telegraph* and the *Sunday Post* as well as *The Beano*, *The Dandy*, *Oor Wullie*, *The Broons* and *Commando*. This building was designed in the style of an American red stone, steel-reinforced office block and was built in 1904-06. A tube allowed messages to be sent by compressed air to and from their offices in nearby Bank Street. A nine-storey tower extension in the same style was added in 1960. Staff were moved out in 2013 when the building underwent extensive renovation; it reopened to employees in 2017 and is now able to accommodate 600 staff though the actual number of employees is much less.

Tram No. 56, outside the Albert Institute on a special service carrying football fans to Dens Park, is rounding the curve in Euclid Crescent which forms a crescent shape around three sides of the High School. This was one of a quartet of trams built by the corporation between 1923 and 1925.

A quintet of trams lined up in Panmure Street alongside the Albert Institute. Extra trams for football fans were run from Albert Square and during the match they queued in Panmure Street, awaiting homeward-bound fans from Dens Park. The Albert Institute behind them was designed by Sir George Gilbert Scott in 1865-67 and a suitable site was obtained at a cost of £8,000 (£825,000 in today's money) but by the time the western half of the building had been completed the money subscribed had been used up. The Free Library Act was shortly afterwards adopted by the inhabitants of Dundee and the ground floor of the building was opened as a Lending and Reference Library. However, an extension to complete the central part of the building was designed by Dundee architect David Mackenzie and built in 1872; the final, eastern part of the building was completed by the City Architect, William Alexander, in 1887. The Institute now included a museum and art gallery and the whole building cost upwards of £20,000 (around £1.85 million today). It was later retitled the McManus Galleries in honour of Maurice McManus, Lord Provost from 1962 to 1967. After a refurbishment in 2010 it is now formally known as 'The McManus: Dundee's Art Gallery and Museum'.

The Central Fire Station in West Bell Street was built in 1900 at a cost of around £8,000 (about £805,000 today) and had accommodation for eight married men and their families. The brigade received its first steam fire engine in 1900, when the new station opened, and its first motor engine in 1911, but the last horses weren't sold off until 1917. In 1970 this West Bell Street Station was closed and the building was subsequently demolished, the brigade moving to new premises in Blackness Road. In 1975 the brigades of Angus, Perthshire and Kinross were amalgamated to form Tayside Fire Brigade, now Tayside Fire and Rescue Services.

The Sheriff Court House in West Bell Street was designed by architect George Angus in 1833, but only the east pavilion was built owing to funds running out. The scheme was completed in 1863 by Dundee's Town Architect William Scott. A western pavilion was demolished in 1974, which spoiled the symmetry of the building, and a new court was created behind the façade of the eastern pavilion in 1979-81. The court was refurbished and extended between 1993 and 1996. The prison, out of sight behind the Court House, was completed in 1834 and remained the burgh gaol until 1927. In 1977 it was demolished to make way for the new Tayside regional police headquarters. The building at the end of the street is part of Gilroy Sons & Co. Ltd.'s massive Tay Bridge jute works, built in 1865. It now contains student accommodation.

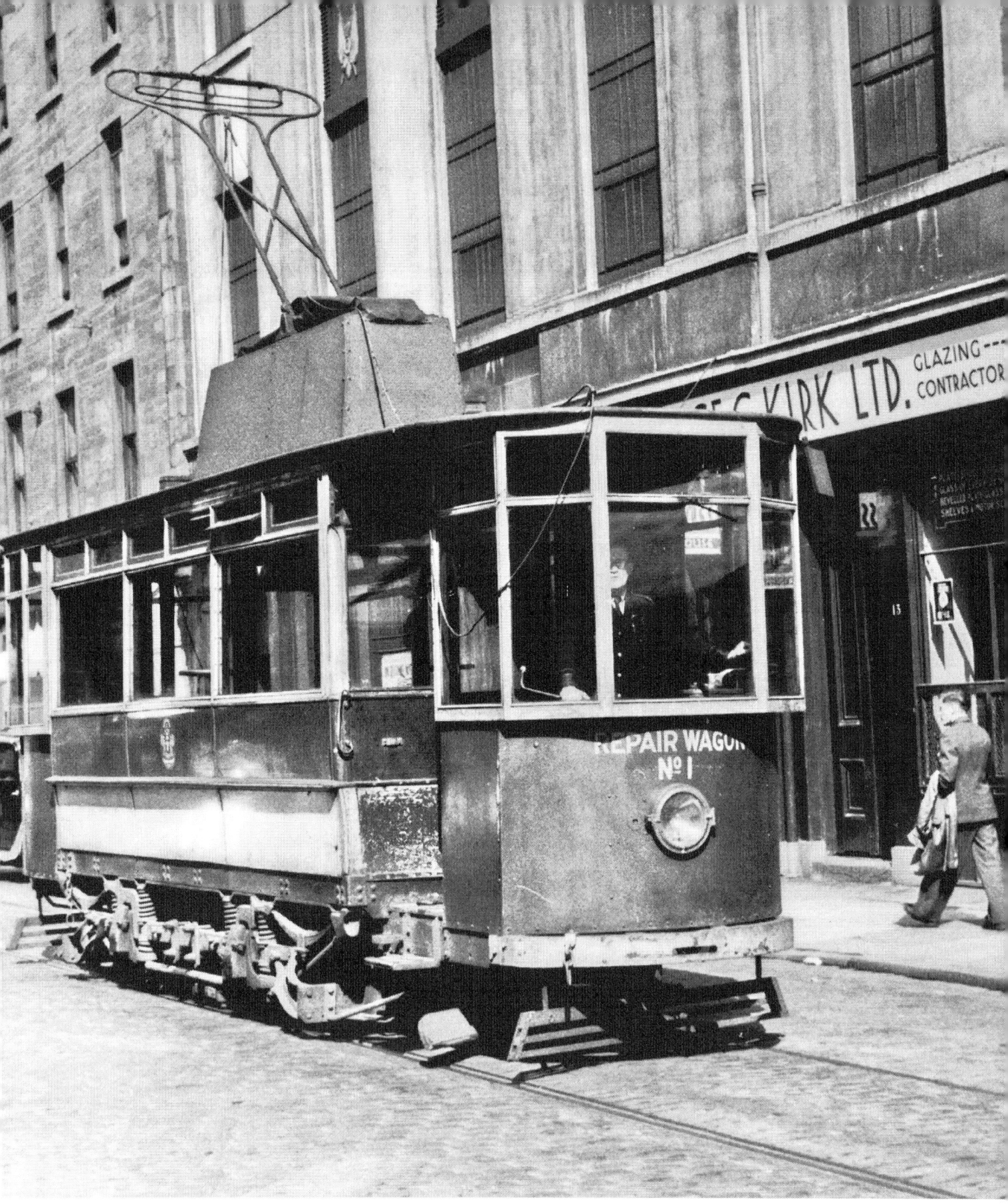

This interesting vehicle, photographed in North Lindsay Street in September 1954, began life as one of a batch of six double-deck covered trams delivered to Dundee Corporation in 1907. In 1935 two of them were cut down and converted for use as repair wagons numbered RW1 and RW2. When the tramway system closed in 1956 RW1 (pictured here) was one of two cars offered for preservation but no suitable storage site could be found and so they were both scrapped along with the rest of the fleet.

This photograph of Overgate was taken looking eastwards towards the Old Steeple. Note the narrowness of the street. As early as 1910 the City Plan had proposed that these eighteenth and nineteenth century buildings should be demolished and the area redeveloped, but this didn't come about until the 1960s when the Overgate Centre was built.

This photograph was taken, probably in the 1950s, from just east of Union Street and looking towards the High Street. Tally Street is in the foreground, Couties Wynd on the right, while the men's outfitter section of Draffen's department store is on the corner of Whitehall Street with Ewings opposite on the far corner. The next street beyond on the right (hidden by the bus) is Crichton Street, after which the buildings flanking the nearside of City Square stand out into the High Street. The large bulk of the Clydesdale Bank can be seen at the far end of the High Street, behind the tram. The steeple rising above the other buildings belongs to St Paul's Episcopal Cathedral. The church opened for worship on 13 December 1855, having cost £14,000 to build (around £1.25 million today). It was raised to the status of Cathedral of Brechin Diocese in 1905. The spire rises to the height of 220 feet.

Another view of the Nethergate, probably taken in the 1920s and again looking eastwards. The buildings on the right are all still there apart from the small building behind the lamppost and the four-windowed building next to it; these have been replaced by a modern block which houses the Nethergate Business Centre and a Tesco Express. The tall building on the near corner of Union Street is the former Russell's Royal Temperance Hotel and facing it across Union Street is the former Trades House, now the Trades House Bar. The nearer steeple with the clock is the Town House and the other, which is at the far end of the High Street, is St Paul's Episcopal Cathedral.

The Nethergate was originally known as the Fluckergait, named after a type of fish, and stretched from the High Street to the Perth Road. It still does so, but its progress is now interrupted by the West Marketgait Inner Ring Road which would today cut across the picture immediately beyond Meadowside St Paul's Church, with its 167 foot high spire. This picture dates from before 1936 which is when Green's Playhouse, with its art deco tower, was opened next to the church. It burned down in 1995, but a Mecca bingo hall built in its place features a similar tower.

This picture shows the buildings immediately beyond those seen above, in a 1950s view along Nethergate towards the Queens Hotel, which can be seen above the outgoing tram which is heading to Balgay Road via Hilltown. The oncoming tram, No. 46, is one of the batch built by Hurst Nelson in 1920 and shows a destination indicator for Maryfield via High Street. The two towers on the right belong to St Enoch's church which was built in 1874. All the buildings in the foreground were demolished when the Overgate Centre and the Inner Ring Road were built; St Enoch's itself was demolished in the late 1960s and its site is now occupied by the Bank of Scotland.

Opposite: The Angus Hotel in Nethergate was built in the first phase of the Overgate development and was opened by Scottish and Newcastle Breweries on 2 March 1964. It was a prestigious building, finished in granite, marble and Norwegian quartz, and was regarded as the best hotel in Dundee for many years; you were expected to dress up if you went in!

In 1996 the Overgate centre's owners, TBI, submitted proposals to the council for a new, redeveloped shopping centre just as the hotel's owners, Mount Charlotte Thistle Hotels had started to redecorate the hotel. They eventually came to an agreement for an undisclosed sum and the hotel closed only two months later. It was demolished in 1998 and part of the Overgate Shopping Centre now occupies the site.

The New Electric Theatre provided by Mr J. Bannister Howard of London was opened on 23 December 1910 by Baillie J. A. Mackay, who said the great feature of this type of entertainment was its educational aspect, and that it might not be very long before something of the same kind might be introduced into the schools. The theatre had a capacity of 500. It was demolished when the Inner Ring Road sliced across Nethergate and a Debenham's store was opened on the site.

Opposite above: This location at the end of Nethergate and beginning of Perth Road was one of the fashionable areas of the city, occupied mainly by businessmen and their families. The house on the right of the picture, named 'Caird Rest', was donated to the community by jute baron Sir James Key Caird, who also gave the city Caird Hall and Caird Park. It opened in 1912 'for the purposes of a place of rest and recreation for aged persons'. It was later used by Dundee University and is now a restaurant named '172 At The Caird'. The picture is full of activity: notice the coalman with his horse and cart loaded with 1cwt (51 kilo) sacks of coal toiling up the road, the cart on the left going downhill with empty coal sacks.

Opposite below: In this 1950s photograph Tram No. 49, dating from the early 1920s, is toiling up the hill past the gardens of University College on the western fringes of Nethergate, bound for West Park on Perth Road. 'Queen's Hotel' is still painted on the facing gable. Still in business today under the same name, the hotel opened in 1878. It was sited in this particular location in anticipation of a new railway station being built nearby following the opening of the Tay Railway Bridge that same year but to the proprietors' chagrin the Tay Bridge Station was actually sited some distance away, near the waterfront. Winston Churchill stayed at the hotel on many occasions when he was the Liberal MP for Dundee between 1908 and 1922.

Perth Road is a continuation of Nethergate and passengers are enjoying a ride on the open top deck of these 1900/02-built trams. Note the one-horse hackney carriage on the right. Millers Wynd runs off to the right between the shops of William Coupar & Co, bakers, on the nearside and James Aitken & Son, grocers and provision merchants, on the far side. On the right, the nearest building has been demolished to build the Millers Wynd Car Park but the block on the far side of Millers Wynd is still completely intact; in fact, the total view is remarkably unchanged today. The tower seen in the distance above the rooftops belonged to George Shaw Aitken's Ryehill United Presbyterian church which opened in 1880 and was converted into nineteen flats in 1987.

Angus Ogilvy & Sons, canvas manufacturers and rope and sail makers, built the Tay Rope Works around 1823. This was taken over by William Lawson & Sons in 1863 and by 1930 they had become the largest producer of jute ropes in Scotland. However, a serious fire in 1937 caused £12,300 (about £690,000 today) worth of damage. Flames shooting skywards attracted thousands of onlookers to the scene. At one point the adjoining jute works and a big oil store were in danger. Every member of Dundee Fire Brigade and every available machine were called out and it took two hours for the fire to be brought under control. Parts of the building were demolished in 1985 and the site of the works has since been developed into houses and flats.

These two trams working the Maryfield to Ninewells service are at the Ninewells terminus, east of Invergowrie Drive on Perth Road. Tram No. 5 was one of the original batch of ten bogie trams delivered in 1900 from the Electric Railway and Tramway Carriage Works at Preston; it was eventually rebuilt as a fully-enclosed four-wheel car. Its companion, which appears to be No. 46, was similarly built as an open-top tram in 1902 by Milnes, Voss & Co. of Birkenhead.

Double-deck open-top Tram No.16, working the Maryfield to Ninewells route, has arrived at the sylvian Ninewells terminus and is pictured with its crew of a driver, conductor and another man who is possibly a ticket inspector. No.16 was one of the original batch of trams bought by Dundee Corporation in 1900/02.

This area known as the West Port was a continuation of Overgate from South Tay Street to where the road divided into Hawkhill (left) and Brook Street (right). There is not, nor ever has been, a West Port exactly here; the real West Port used to stand in the Overgate and all traffic going westward went through it, though it was demolished in 1757 because it had become a hindrance to this traffic. Major alterations were made to the junction in the 1960s when Dundee's Inner Ring Road was constructed. Brook Street was renamed Hawkhill, was realigned and was converted into a main road that swept away old housing. The original Hawkhill road was renamed Old Hawkhill and, truncated, is no longer a through road for vehicles. The building in the centre of the picture, still standing, bears a datestone of 1823 and the clock above it shows 1864. The left half of the building is the Globe pub and the right half is the premises of J. McArtney, ironmongers.

Hawkhill acquired its name because hawkers (travelling pedlars) were allowed to ply their wares there. This view of the beginning of the road was taken from the West Port and is older than the above picture because the first building on Hawkhill has not yet been rebuilt. Almost all the children in the picture are barefooted; Hawkhill was one of the poorest and most deprived areas of the city.

Small Wynd is a short distance up Hawkhill beyond the West Port and Wallace's Pend, seen here, was typical of housing conditions behind the main street. The newspapers of the early 1900s were full of reports of theft, assault and violent conduct in the district, but these were not confined to the Hawkhill: there were several other badly deprived areas in the city, including Hilltown, Murraygate, the area around the Greenmarket, and parts of Lochee.

This 1907 picture looks back down the hill towards the West Port. The street is a mixture of late eighteenth and nineteenth century buildings, those built from 1850 onwards being taller. Nothing remains of this scene today.

John Soutar's tobacconist corner shop was at 72 Hawkhill. The posters around the doorway indicate the political stories of the time; the *Advertiser*'s big story is of a Tory Party revolt against their leader, Arthur Balfour. This dates the picture to around 1907/08. The shop was situated on the corner of Park Wynd, a little way up the hill from West Port. The stone setts remain but the shop has been demolished and the area is now part of the Abertay Universities buildings.

The Grocer and Spirit Merchant shop of William Craig Jackson at 208 Hawkhill was located on the left-hand side of the road going up the hill, just below Miller's Wynd. Its site is now a grass verge next to a sign leading to the Mid Wynd Industrial Estate.

This was Alfred Fairweather's shop at 276 Hawkhill; he seems to have a particular affection for the *Scottish Weekly Record* newspaper!

The junction known as the Sinderins where Hawkhill, on the left, joins the westbound Perth Road. Most of the buildings in this Edwardian picture are still standing but the junction has been remodelled, as has the angled building facing the camera.

Ramsay's Pend, near Brook Street, is mentioned in the *Dundee, Perth and Cupar Advertiser* of 3 March 1848 regarding a trial before two JPs when William Doogan, contractor, was accused of allowing 'an accumulation of noxious matter, refuse, dung, etc. in Ramsay's Pend, and pig styes situated there.' The same newspaper followed this up in August with a report that 'Ramsay's Pend was in the same frightful condition, save that the accumulated refuse seemed to have lain for a century untouched. The windows of the houses in this place were generally open, and at most of them might be seen the pale, sickly, sallow features of women, young and old, whose view was bounded by a few dilapidated houses, and the only objects of interest an ashpit and a privy'.

Brook Street is pictured here, running down the left side of the picture towards the West Port. Session Street runs down to the right of the picture to a junction with Guthrie Street. The General Dealer on the corner of Brook Street was Mrs J. McManus. The pub next door was the Celtic Bar and next came James P. Casey, a dealer in 'furniture, left-off clothing, antiquarian and general bookseller, and licensed pawnbroker'. His advertisement in the *Dundeer Courier & Advertiser* said that Mr and Mrs Casey 'will pay good prices in cash for any part of anyone's superfluous wardrobe'. Their wall-painted sign says, 'Furniture & House Furnishings of Every Description Bought, Sold or Exchanged'. In 1909 the licensee of the Celtic Bar placed an advert in the *Evening Telegraph* for several months, which read 'For WORKING MEN ONLY. John Finnegan, Celtic Bar, Brook Street sells Schooners of Beer for 1½d'. A later licensee, William Coupar, became bankrupt in March 1928; the pub's fixtures and fittings were auctioned off and the pub closed down. This section of Brook Street has been altered out of recognition by the construction of the Inner Ring Road. It has been renamed 'Hawkhill' and turned into a dual carriageway.

A 1914 view along Brook Street. Burnett Street enters on the left and Guthrie Street on the right. The works chimneys are, from left to right: Walton Jute Works (demolished); Edward Street Jute Mill (still standing but chimney demolished) and Garden Works; Blyth Street Jute Mill (demolished).

The cart laden with sacks of coal is making the sharp turn from Blackness Road into Blackness Street. The turning into Rosefield Place is just visible in the bottom right of the picture. All the buildings on the right are still standing and the wall beyond the four-storey tenement is the site of the Liff & Benvie Poor House, also known as the West Poor House, which opened in 1864 and closed in 1914, when its buildings were then used by the military during the First World War. After the war the building was taken over by Logie Central School which later became Harris Academy Annexe. The old poorhouse building was demolished and replaced by a new building which opened in 1929 but closed in 1998. It remained unoccupied until It was damaged by fire in 2001 and subsequently demolished. Its site is now occupied by the Balgay Hill Nursery School, St Joseph's Roman Catholic and Victoria Park Primary Schools.

Tram No. 2, built by Electric Railway & Tramway Carriage Works in 1900, is heading for Downfield along Blackness Road, here passing the corner of Victoria Park at the junction of Balgay Road by the corner of the bowling green. The tram was originally open top and received a top cover in 1906-07, but retained its exposed balconies. It was then rebuilt as fully enclosed during 1928-29.

Tram No. 8, similar to the one in the previous picture, standing at the Blackness terminus of the Blackness to Downfield route.

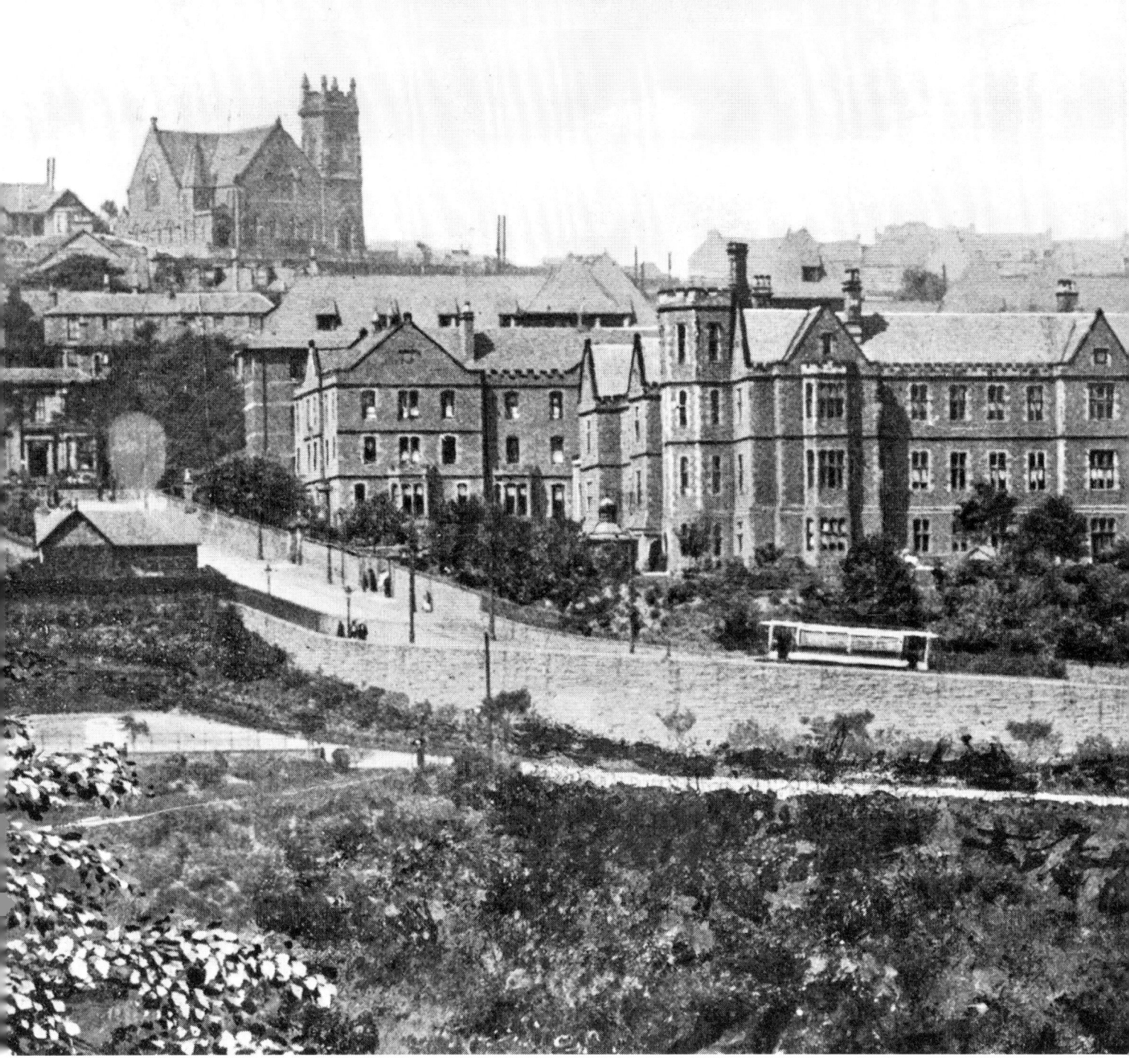

Dundee Royal Infirmary's origins lay in a voluntary dispensary in 1782 and in 1793 it was proposed that an infirmary for indoor patients should be founded. Subsequently, the 56-bed Dundee Infirmary was opened in King Street in 1798. It was granted a Royal Charter in 1819, after which it became known as the Dundee Royal Infirmary and Asylum. In 1820 the asylum was established as a separate entity in its own premises in Albert Street and the hospital gained its official title of Dundee Royal Infirmary. Despite raising capacity to 120 beds in the 1820s the ever-expanding population of Dundee meant that by the middle of the nineteenth century the King Street premises were no longer adequate. In 1852 work started on a new site in Barrack Road and the building opened in 1855. The new hospital proved to be more expensive to build than anticipated, with the £14,000 (£1.6 million today) raised for the project by public subscription failing to cover the building cost. On top of this, the Normandy stone around the building's windows proved unable to cope with the climate and within thirty years had to be replaced at a cost of

around £5,000 (around £500,000 today). The new building, seen here around 1913, was originally built to accommodate 220 patients, but this was extended several times as the hospital expanded its services. Prior to the creation of the National Health Service in 1948, the infirmary depended heavily on the generosity of wealthy benefactors such as Sir James Baxter and other textile magnates. During the First World War part of the infirmary became a military hospital. A specialist Neurosurgery Department was opened in 1966 and in the 1970s the hospital became one of the first in the United Kingdom to acquire a CAT scan head scanner. Dundee Royal Infirmary, often shortened to DRI, was Dundee's main hospital and a major teaching hospital until the opening of Ninewells Hospital in 1974, but after a prolonged debate as to whether DRI or Maryfield hospital should be closed, the axe fell on DRI in 1998. The original buildings and main later additions have been converted into housing and renamed Regents Gardens. This project was completed in 2008.

Dudhope Castle, situated on the southern edge of Dudhope Park, was originally built in the late thirteenth century by the Scrymgeour family, hereditary constables of the burgh. Circular towers were added in 1580 but these were demolished in the eighteenth century. In 1668 King Charles II ignored the claims of the rightful heir, John Scrimgeour of Kirkton, and made a grant of Dudhope Castle to Charles Maitland, a younger brother of the 1st Duke of Lauderdale, but Maitland sold the castle in 1684 to John Graham of Claverhouse, better known as 'Bonnie Dundee'. Claverhouse was killed in 1689 during the Battle of Killiecrankie; because he had supported the Stuart cause his lands were forfeited and granted to Archibald Douglas in 1694. The Douglas family were the last of occupants of Dudhope Castle, in residence there until about 1790 when they moved to Dudhope House. In 1792-93 the castle was rented out to the British Woollen Company in an attempt to use it as a woollen

factory, but the plan never came to fruition. In 1795 the park and the grounds were leased to the Board of Ordnance who used it as a barracks until 1879. In 1854 the Town Council had acquired a sub-lease of the castle grounds for use as recreational facilities, ending in November 1890. At this time the Earl of Home wished to develop the grounds for terraced housing but instead the Corporation of Dundee, as the council had by then become, acquired the estate for £31,700 (around £3.4 million today) and opened as Dudhope Park in 1895. The castle was later occupied by the Ministry of Works and used as a military barracks during both the 1914-1918 and 1939-1945 wars. In 1958 the castle passed to the Corporation which initially wished to demolish it as it had fallen into disrepair. However, from 1985 to 1988 it was redeveloped as offices and a conference centre and also houses the University of Abertay Dundee Business School.

The original cannon sited at Dudhope Castle was said to be a captured piece from the siege of Sevastopol, 1854-55. It was replaced at least twice due to wear. This particular cannon, photographed around 1880, was presented in 1872 and erected in the Barrack Square, immediately in front of the officers' quarters and overlooking the town. A wooden house containing the apparatus connected with the gun, including the exploder and the galvanometer, was situated about 50 feet away. It was connected by an electric wire with the Observatory on Calton Hill, Edinburgh, to synchronise with the Observatory's time. The cannon was initially fired daily at one o'clock but this ceased in 1916 so as not to disturb patients at the nearby Royal Infirmary, some of whom were suffering from shell shock. Daily firing was never resumed. After 1924 it was only fired on New Year's Day and Armistice Day. The cannon was last fired in 1936; it is now believed lost.

The children's playground in Barrack Park, c. 1914, with the Royal Infirmary in the background and Dudhope Castle on the right. It was believed that the two cannons in the picture had been captured from the Russian army during the Crimean War.

The entrance to Barrack Park on Lochee Road, with Dudhope Castle in the middle background and the faint outline of Dundee Royal Infirmary visible in the distance. The stone pillars guarding the park entrance are still *in situ* today but the elaborate lamps on their tops are no more. Nowadays, the tramlines have also disappeared and so has the building of the Park & Pleasance Brewery on the right of the picture which has been replaced by the Ballingall Industrial Estate.

Smellie's Lane leads from Lochee Road opposite Dudhope Park, down through Henderson's Wynd to Guthrie Street. The tenement in the picture is long gone, replaced by a Magnet Kitchens showroom, and only the stone setts and the wall on the far side of Lochee Road are left to identify the location of the picture.

Cleghorn Street, seen here around 1912, lies west of Dudhope Park and connects Lochee Road with City Road. The street slopes down at its lower end towards City Road but nowhere near as precipitously as it appears in this picture, which was taken at its junction with Benvie Road. The 1895-built Victorian buildings on both sides of the street look almost the same today. The only major difference is W. C. Ramsay's shop on the corner which, unlike its modern successor, the Cleghorn Licensed Convenience Store, combined the roles of newsagent and chemist.

The land on which Balgay Park is situated to the north-west of the city was bought by the city fathers with the intention of improving the health of mill workers who lived and worked in poor conditions. It was intended as a counterpart of Baxter Park in the east of the city, which had been the gift of Sir David Baxter, but Balgay Park was paid for out of additional local taxation. The park is separated from the old Western Necropolis by a deep crevasse which is crossed by this elegant three-span cast-iron bridge with a principal arch of 80 feet, seen here around 1910. The shield on the arch bears the town's arms and the following inscription: 'Balgay Hill Recreation Grounds, provided by the Community of Dundee for The Use of the People and Opened 20 September 1871'.

The footway on the bridge in Balgay Park was originally constructed of timber and had a width of 8 feet. The bridge is about 42 feet above the roadway. By 1902 three people had committed suicide by jumping from it and a proposal to place three strands of barbed wire horizontally along the bridge on brackets adjoining each parapet to 'ensure greater safety to the public' was approved and then rescinded. However, to prevent further casualties, the 3½ feet high rail was heightened in 1904 to 6 feet by the addition of ornate wire fencing. The bridge is seen here around 1910 but by the 1920s it had fallen into disrepair largely because of a dispute between council departments over who was responsible for its upkeep. In 1929 the bridge was repaired and strengthened with a reinforced concrete deck. It was restored again in 2002.

Logie Garden City, situated on Dundee's south-east facing slopes beneath Balgay Hill, is bounded by Blackness Road, Balgay Road, Scott Street and Glenagnes Road. It was the first municipal housing scheme to take advantage of the 1919 Housing and Town Planning (Scotland) Act and was designed to relieve the city's overcrowded slums. The scheme of 250 apartment houses originally incorporated a municipal heating system which supplied central heating and hot water to each house, with a communal laundry built in Scott Street. It was made up of three and four-roomed houses, built according to the ideals of the Garden City Movement. Known as maisonettes, there were four flats in each housing block, two upper and two lower, each with its own front door and with a small allotment. Opened in 1920 by Lord Provost William Don, the proposed street names had been Victoria for the main avenue, with streets on either side being named after the First World War generals and admirals Haig, Beatty, Allenby, Rawlinson and Kitchener. However, in the end, the agreed names were Logie for the main avenue and Sycamore, Elm, Lime, Ashbank and Birchwood for the side roads. The estate was designated as an outstanding conservation area in 1991.

Dundee Law is a hill which is nowadays in the centre of Dundee due to housebuilding. The highest point in the city at 572 feet above sea level, the Law is what remains of a volcanic sill, created 400 million years ago. During the Iron Age it was the site of a Pictish settlement and Roman pottery has also been found here. On 13 April 1689 Viscount 'Bonnie' Dundee raised the Royal Stuart standard here, marking the beginning of the first Jacobite rising. The photograph is looking in the general direction of Lochee on the left. St Thomas's Parish Church (nowadays Balgay Parish Church) is in the right foreground with Tullidelph Road running past its nearside. This is soon crossed by City Road on its way northwards from Blackness to Lochee. The houses and villas in the picture all appear to have survived but not so the four and five-storied tenements. The two large Gothic-styled buildings in the centre of the picture are St Joseph's Convent opened in 1892.

Tram No. 40 is being passed by its nemesis as it pauses by Lochee railway station. This was the last of seven trams built by Hurst Nelson in 1920. The family on the left are standing in the doorway of Attilio Dellanzo's fish and chip shop on the corner of Logie Street and Muirton Street; the premises are now A1 Stores. Part of Lochee High Street is visible looking through the bridge arch.

Lochee Station was designed by Edinburgh architect Sir James Gowans for the Dundee & Newtyle Railway and opened on 10 June 1861. It was a two platform station with a passing loop and the main station building was on the northbound platform where Caledonian Railway No. 179 is standing with a passenger train in this 1906 picture. The line was closed to passenger traffic on 10 January 1955 but remained in operation for goods until 1967. The station building was converted in 1972 and extended to the south to become the Lochee Burns Club.

Lochee Public Baths, opened in 1894, was one of a number erected in the late nineteenth century as part of measures to improve the city's unenviable health record, and was a gift to the community by the Cox brothers, owners of the vast Camperdown Works in Lochee. It was built at 45/47 High Street and 2 St Mary's Lane, in a Jacobean Renaissance style. What appears to be an octagonal tower on the far end of the building is actually the tower of Lochee Catholic Church of the Immaculate Conception which adjoins the baths. The swimming pool originally had a diving board and changing cubicles surrounding the poolside. Only females were allowed to use these cubicles; the male swimmers had to use a communal changing room nicknamed the Dungeon. The swimming pool hall was refurbished in 1979, 1989 and 1994, though the original wrought iron roof trusses with cast iron struts have been retained.

In this view of the High Street in the late 1930s not a single building on the left side of the street has survived.

A 1950s view looking towards the centre of Lochee. The nearest block on the right seen above the Luxor lorry, has been demolished and replaced by an unsympathetic modern block; the next two blocks are intact but the same fate has befallen the rest of the buildings on that side of the road up to the junction. The stylish four-storey buildings at the junction have survived, unlike the buildings lining the left-hand side of the street which have all been replaced by modern three-storey concrete blocks.

The centre of Lochee where Methven Street (alongside the United Free East Church) and Bright Street join the High Street. The people streaming down Methven Street have come from the Camperdown Works which is situated at the end of the street. The nearest shops are Peter Mitchell's Wines and Spirits and J. C. Hunter. The wagonette's registration letters of TS denotes that it is a local vehicle.

Workers streaming out of Cox Brothers' Camperdown Works on their dinner break. In 1810 the Cox (originally Cock) family firm had become a pioneer in the manufacture of jute cloth. In 1849 it began construction of the Camperdown Works in Lochee, starting with both a power loom mill and a separate handloom mill; in 1857 it commenced building the High Mill. This was

completed in 1865 with a calendaring (finishing) mill. Eventually the works covered a 35-acre site. It was the largest jute mill in the world and by 1900 employed more than 5,000 workers. The entire works closed in 1981 and much of the site has been redeveloped with housing and entertainment facilities.

The descent into Lochee High Street from the west, seen from close to its junction with Liff Road. The church with the ornate tower is Lochee East United Free church which was demolished in 1960 to make way for a Woolworth's store. Apart from the church, nearly all the buildings are still standing today.

Looking in the opposite direction to the previous picture, and now in the late 1930s, all the buildings on both sides of the road as far as the tram are still standing. The tram in the distance is about to take the right-hand bend to its terminus just past the junction with Liff Road and the building in the distance in the centre is Liff Road School.

The buildings in this *c.* 1912 view of the end of Liff Road, looking towards its junction with the end of the High Street, have been completely swept away under the northern junction of Lochee High Street with the Lochee Bypass. Trams running along the High Street went a little way past the junction as far as their terminus at Liff Road School.

The new Liff Road elementary school at Lochee was opened in 1891. With a capacity of 662, its construction had been made necessary because of the overcrowded state of the other public schools in Lochee. The plans also provided for future accommodation for 230 additional pupils. However, this never came about and the school was demolished in 1972 to make way for the A90 Lochee Bypass.

Irish immigrants started to arrive in Dundee around 1825 and within thirty years the population of Irish-born Dundonians had grown to 14,000. Lochee, blighted by poverty and poor quality housing, was where the bulk of them settled, to be close to their workplace which was usually the Camperdown Works. Atholl Street, seen here, was nicknamed 'Tipperary', usually abbreviated to 'Tip'. The Camperdown Works can be seen in the background.

Cox's Stack is a 282-foot-high chimney that was constructed in 1865/66 as part of the vast Camperdown Works. It was modelled on an Italian campanile.

Byron Street is a long road on the north side of Dundee Law, connecting Loons Road in the west with the streets of Hilltown in the east. This photograph was taken looking eastwards with the crossroads with Lawton Road just visible in the distance, marked with signposts. The short row of three bungalows is still there, standing incongruously amid the semi-detached houses.

This inn, built in 1870, is Birkhill Inn (known locally as the 'Birkie') and is easily recognisable behind the restaurant that has been built along the whole of the frontage. It is well-known locally for its award-winning 'Birkie' Steak Pies.

Returning towards the city centre, Hilltown was once a separate barony outside the burgh of Dundee but in 1697 it was purchased by the town and annexed. It was originally called Bonnet Hill as many of its inhabitants were engaged in bonnet making, but by the late eighteenth century the majority of the city's handloom weavers were concentrated in this area. This early twentieth century view is looking up the precipitous Hilltown. The hill was so steep that a pool of horses were kept at the foot to provide extra muscle power when needed by carters. The tenement on the right-hand side of the street behind the central lamppost is still standing but everything else in the picture has been demolished.

This photograph was taken a little further up the hill than the previous one. The church-like building on the left is the Progress Masonic Halls, known as the 'Proggie'. Trams couldn't operate on this lower, steeper, part of the hill but in 1902 tramlines were laid from Constitution Street which is nearer the top of the hill, and turned left to head for Downfield. Six single-deck trams were purchased specially to operate this service.

Alexander Street is situated near the top of Hilltown. This 1911 picture looks down the hill towards Dens Road, with North Wellington Street crossing in the foreground. Most of the tenements were erected in the 1880s but practically nothing at all remains today. A modern industrial estate has been built on the site of the first block of tenements on the left-hand side of Alexander Street but the first part of the second block of tenements, on the further side of North Ellen Street, still stands. On the righthand side of the street there are nowadays blocks of very modern flats all the way down the hill; these have replaced the Maxwelltown, Carnegie and Jamaica tower blocks of flats that were built in 1968 but demolished in 2011. The part of North Wellington Street on the right of the picture no longer exists; nowadays a children's playground is in its place, with Our Lady's Roman Catholic Primary School and its grounds lying beyond.

When Dundonians talk about the 'tap o' the hill' they are talking about this area at the top of Hilltown. Its most outstanding landmark is the clock, which was donated to the community in 1900 by councillor Baillie Charles Barrie, who became Lord Provost of Dundee between 1902 and 1905.

In this picture of the top of the hill, Main Street runs off to the right of Patterson's public house (nowadays the Bowbridge Bar), Strathmartine Road runs to the left of the clock and Mains Road runs to its right to join Clepington Road, with the foundries, carpet works and tenements of Fairmile visible in the distance. All the buildings here have survived.

The Rosebank Bar at 77 Rosebank Street in the Hilltown area is nowadays Tam's Bar and the buildings on the left of the picture have been replaced by the McGonagall House Care Home.

Strathmartine Road begins at the top of Hilltown and runs all the way up to Downfield. This house named 'Fernlea', at 476 Strathmartine Road, was owned by Alexander Ross, a builder. The house is instantly recognisable today though the outbuilding at the side has been replaced by a garage and the hedge by a low garden wall. Judging by the milk churn on the trap and the leather bag carried by the man standing in the road, they are on a milk delivery round.

Edward Cotogno (1885-1922) and his wife Norah Mitchell (1893-1980) owned this confectionery shop at 461 Strathmartine Road. The photograph was taken in 1919 and these shop premises are still there, occupied by Nicoll's Rosebank Bakery.

Wedderburn Street is on the right and the turning into Francis Street is just visible on the left in this view of a tram coming down Strathmartine Road from Downfield. The tram looks to be No. 63, a covered tram with balconies that were open to the elements, which had been bought in 1908. The view along the road looks almost identical today, though a small grassed area and a block of modern three-storey apartments today occupy the place of the building half-hidden behind the trees on the right.

The view looking down Clepington Road from this junction with Strathmartine Road looks the same today. Clepington Road was the main access to the two estates of Easter Clepington and Wester Clepington which were divided by part of the old Glamis Road which runs up from Dens Road.

In 1954 U.K. Time Company changed its name to Timex. The company recruited workers throughout the 1960s, offering them help in moving to Dundee and with housing. In the mid 1960s production changed from non-jewelled watches to the production of the American Polaroid Company's first low-priced instant-picture camera. These automatic machine tools were installed at its factory in Harrison Road, north of the A90 Kingsway. Industrial relations were often fraught and the factory closed in 1993 after a bitter dispute between the management and the workforce.

In 1929 the National Cash Register Company (NCR) introduced the Class 3000 accounting machine following its acquisition of the Ellis Adding-Typewriter Company. This was an accounting machine that incorporated a typewriter. NCR was acquired by AT&T in 1991 and this factory at Kingsway West closed in 1986 when production was transferred to Hungary.

A tram heading along Strathmartine Road on its way to Downfield and crossing the roundabout with Kingsway, which is nowadays the city's A90 Outer Ring Road.

Two early twentieth century views from Kingsway Circus looking north along Strathmartine Road towards Downfield, with the Sidlaw Hills rising behind the village. The buildings on the left of the picture look identical today.

Baldovan Station was opened in 1831 on the Dundee and Newtyle Railway, whose original line included three rope-worked inclined planes and a tunnel through Dundee Law. However, in 1861 a deviation was opened to avoid Law Tunnel and Law Incline, allowing the line to be worked throughout by steam locomotives. In 1905 the station was renamed Baldovan and Downfield. It was located behind the Downfield Tavern (nowadays the Downfield Hotel) near where Strathmartine Road crossed the railway. In 1907 Downfield became the northern limit of Dundee Tramways. It took a more direct route and quicker than the railway, serving a much higher population. In this 1908 photograph, the tram is at the terminus and beyond it Strathmartine Road bends round to the left to cross the railway on an overbridge which is just visible on the left of the picture. After closure of the railway in 1955 the station and goods yard were cleared and a modern block of flats was built on the site.

The large building in the background is the Dundee Industrial School for Boys at Baldovan which was opened in 1878 on Strathmartine Road. It provided accommodation for 200 boys aged from eight to sixteen. The school had transferred from a smaller site at Ward Road which had opened in 1861 as a reformatory, receiving children who were committed by magistrates for a period of detention, and also for poor and destitute children. Following a decline in numbers placed at the school, it finally closed in 1983. The site is now covered by a modern housing estate.

Two views looking towards the tram terminus at Downfield, which was alongside the railway station's coal yard. Baldovan Road is on the right, and the entire location is now buried under a roundabout.

Summer of 1951 at Downfield, where one of the trams on the cross-city Downfield to Blackness service has left the terminus in Strathmartine Road and is heading back to Blackness. This cross-city service was suspended on 26 November 1955 and never reintroduced, the entire tramway system being shut down on 25 October 1956.

The foundation stone of St Luke's Episcopal Church, at the junction of St Luke's Road and Baldovan Road in Downfield, was laid in 1901. It seated 250 and consisted of a nave, chancel and vestry, with provision for a tower and spire to be added subsequently (which was never carried out).

Americanmuir Road has nothing to do with the United States of America. It was originally merely a road to Meric Muir and it is believed that it only gained its transatlantic-sounding title when it was engulfed by the expansion of Dundee. It connects Macalpine Road in the west with Strathmartine Road in the east and is nowadays lined in the most part with a mixture of modern houses and bungalows.

These rows of single-storey cottages at Trottick Mains, located off Claverhouse Road and photographed around 1907, were originally thatched and were built in the 1790s for workers at the Trottick flax spinning mill where Mr Scott, the proprietor, played the fiddle while supervising his workforce. Its early water-powered mill was superseded by the steam-powered mills of central Dundee and the cottages were acquired by the adjacent bleaching company of Thomas Collier and Company. Bleaching was the last stage in the production of linen cloth.

Heading south-eastwards from Downfield towards Victoria Road, Ann Street ran from the Hillbank Works on Hillbank Street across to Hilltown Road, whose tenements can be seen in the distance. The whole length of the street was built up, largely with a range of small shops, but they were all swept away in the early 1970s and the scene today from the same viewpoint at the corner of Nelson Street is of blocks of flats on the left-hand side of the road and Our Lady's Roman Catholic Primary School on the right.

Dundonald Street runs in an easterly direction from Dens Road/Arklay Street to the Manhattan jute works. This picture was taken at the corner of Clepington Street sometime around 1911 but, apart from the former Dura Street jute mills building seen in the distance, only the building on the left of the picture nearest the camera survives, now the Airlie Arms. The building on the right with the bell appears to be the rear entrance to the Rashiewell Works which was built in 1855 as Clepington Power Loom Works. This is now the premises of a cash and carry.

Manhattan New Mill, a single-storey jute spinning and weaving works, was built in Dundonald Street, off Dens Road, in 1873/74 for the firm of F. S. Sandeman & Sons Ltd. This became part of Jute Industries Ltd in 1921, an amalgamation of many of the Dundee jute companies including Cox Brothers (Camperdown Works), Thomas Bell & Sons (Belmont Works), Gilroy & Sons (Tay Works) and J. & A. D. Grimond (Bowbridge Works). It changed its name to Sidlaw Industries Ltd in 1971 and to Sidlaw Group plc in 1981. Spinning at the Manhattan mill ended in 1995 and the building is now occupied by several small businesses.

Ogilvie Street runs from halfway along Dundonald Street southwards to meet Dura Street. This photograph is taken from Dundonald Street. All the buildings in view on the left side of the street have survived. While the shop and tenements on the right are still standing, the works building beyond it has been demolished and replaced with modern three-storey tenements. The works were the Constable Jute Works of Malcolm, Ogilvie & Company, built around 1850. By 1864 the firm had 220 looms and 4,000 spindles and employed 1,000 workers. In 1970 the company moved to the old Dundee Linen Works in Constitution Street, renaming the factory the Constable Works. The old factory in the picture was subsequently demolished.

Malcolm Street, looking towards its junction with Ogilvie Street. The tenements on the left still run the entire length of the street but those on the right have been truncated in the area of the shop to create a small grassed area. The Constable Works are at the end of the street.

Harry Walker came to Dundee from Fife in 1833 from Blebo, Fife and, with his brother John, built Dura Works for spinning jute yarn. In 1873 a new firm of Harry Walker & Sons was formed. This owned Caldrum Works, built in 1872-73, the second biggest jute mill in Dundee. By 1913 the works had been extended to cover 8 acres and had 9,500 spindles. Subsequently, the firm became a part of Jute Industries Ltd. In 1911 the firm's offices were extended forward, integrating the gateposts as partial support for a new first-floor level, though they still remain recognisable today. The mill now houses Bonar Yarns Ltd.

Dens Park, now officially known as Kilmac Stadium, the home of Dundee FC and is situated is only 200 yards from Tannadice Park, home of rivals Dundee United. The club was formed by the merger of two teams, Our Boys and East End, both founded in 1877. Dundee FC was admitted to the Scottish League in 1893 and for a time they played at West Craigie Park (Our Boys' ground) before moving to Carolina Port. In 1898 it leased a plot of farmland at Dens Road and purchased it in 1919, remodelling the ground. The club's record attendance was 43,024 for a Scottish Cup match against Rangers in 1953. A new stand was built behind each goal in 1999, reducing the ground's capacity to 11,850. This card shows a match against Hearts and is postmarked 1906 so it may refer to the 1-1 match played on 21 October 1905 before a crowd of 14,000 spectators.

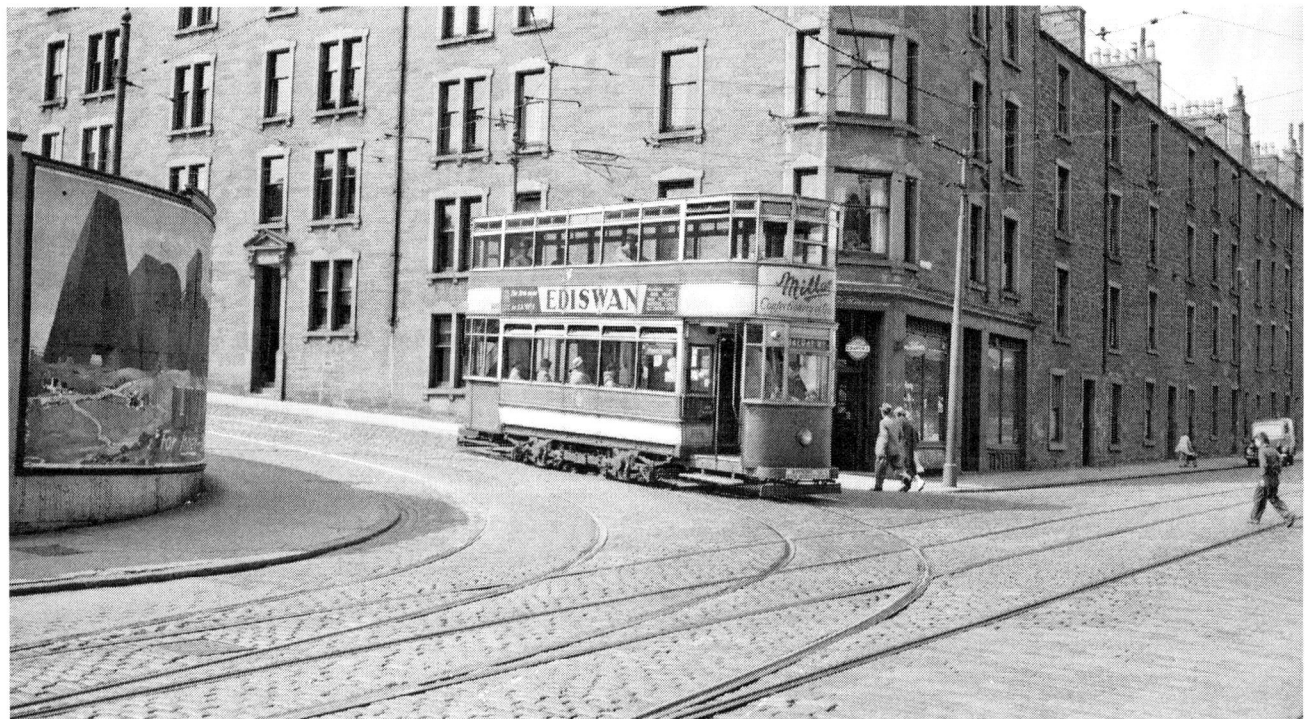

A tram heading for Balgay Road has come down the slope of Main Street and is turning into Dens Road where it would join one of the two tram routes from Downfield which had diverged further north at Coldside. The junction is unchanged today.

This is an 1874 view of what must have been one of the busiest junctions in Dundee before it was swept away in the wake of the 1871 Improvement Act. Hilltown is running downhill past the buildings on the left to its foot at its junction on the right with the Wellgate, while Bucklemaker Wynd is straight ahead, almost hidden behind the horse. By the mid-nineteenth century this narrow street, only 13 feet wide, was daily carrying scores of vehicles going in both directions and, with the construction of the Victoria Bridge over the Dens Burn, it now linked to the Arbroath road via the new Victoria Street, while Dens Road provided access to the north of the city. This led to its rebuilding as Victoria Road (along the same line as the old wynd) with a 60-feet wide carriageway. The Bucklemakers were a branch of the Hammermen, one of the Nine Trades, and made buckles of all kinds.

This picture shows the remodelled junction. Hilltown comes down from the left, the Wellgate steps are on the right and straight ahead is the bottom end of Victoria Road. The only recognisable building seen here is the turreted tenement in the distance to the left of the tram. All the other buildings have been demolished, the ones on the right to make way for the Wellgate Centre, opened in 1977, and those on the left to make way for The Little Theatre and a paved seating area.

Victoria Road was created in 1884 by the major widening of what had been Bucklemaker Wynd. A. & S. Henry's calender finishing works are prominent on the left-hand side with turrets on each end of the building (the tenement across the road was probably designed to match). This firm was founded in Manchester in 1805 and these premises were built in 1874/75. In 1972 the company was taken over by the Titaghur Jute Factory Ltd but in 1983 this went into receivership. The building was converted into private flats in 1997. The nearest buildings along the left-hand side of the road as far as Henry's building have not survived, nor have those on the other side of the road.

This scene is looking in the opposite direction down towards the Wellgate. A. & S. Henry's works is the only survivor of the buildings in the foreground on either side of the road. Trinity Christian Union church on the right has been replaced by modern flats while the buildings beyond the works have been demolished. On the other side of the road all the buildings have been replaced by the Central Library.

The Victoria Brewery, situated at 16/18 Victoria Road, drew its water from the Lady Well, the parent source of the city's water supply. It was built by Margaret Wills in 1876 as part of a development scheme on the site of an earlier brewery established by her late husband. The brewery was later taken on by John Neave & Sons Ltd and went into liquidation in 1910, the brewery, along with the Ladywell Tavern, being offered for sale. The building is still there, although not recognisable from the picture.

This view is barely recognisable today. It is looking up King Street from its Panmure Street end. When the Inner Ring Road of North Marketgait was built in 1973 the nearer tenements on the left of the picture were demolished and became the car park of nearby St Andrew's Church, while all the remainder lie under the ring road. Fortunately, the buildings in view on the right have survived as far as the end of the terrace.

King Street continues beyond the Inner Ring Road until it reaches Dens Brae where this former Upper Dens Mill of Baxter Brothers stands on the left-hand side of the road, at which point it becomes Princes Street. This vast mill was erected in 1865/66 but only the nearest mill building still stands; it was converted into flats in the 1990s. The further building, beyond Weavers Yard, has been demolished and replaced by more flats. The nearer buildings on the right were demolished in 1935 to build an extension to Baxter Brothers' Lower Dens Mills. Baxter Brothers were the biggest linen manufacturers in Dundee and supplied the armed forces with fabrics ranging from heavy sail canvas and tarpaulins to gun covers, biscuit bagging and sailors' gaiters. By 1890 Baxter's was the world's largest linen manufacturer with a workforce of 5,000. Business declined in the 1960s due to overseas competition and the mills closed in 1974.

Princes Street is connected with Victoria Street by Crescent Street and this is where Baxter's opened their half-time school in 1858. The 1833 Factories Act had forbidden the employment of children under nine in the textile industry and the 1844 Act introduced the half-time system of education for child workers from the ages of eight to fourteen. 'Half-timers' were employed in the mills for either ten hours every alternate day, in which case the next day was spent in the mill school, or from 5 a.m. until 11 a.m. at work, with the afternoon until 6 p.m. spent at school. Baxter's school closed in 1905 when it was incorporated into Wallacetown School; Wallacetown Nursery School now occupies its site. The clock tower in the background is of Wallacetown Church of Scotland.

Princes Street was laid out by 1821. A concentration of mills in the area meant that it was once the busiest street outside the centre of Dundee, with over 100 shops. All the buildings on the right of the picture have survived but the ones on the left have been replaced by the Princes Street Car Park.

Graham Place is a small street which connects Princes Street with Robertson Street. The road is located on a hill, which is why the little girl on the right is having to step up high to reach the pavement. Only a few of the buildings in this picture have survived today. The section of tenements on the left with the pointed heads to the windows have been demolished and so have those on the right from the lamppost towards the camera; both have been replaced with modern housing. The shops at the end of the road on the far side of Princes Street have been replaced by the Princes Street Car Park.

Mr and Mrs David Hill McIntosh in the doorway of their bootmaker's shop at 193 Princes Street, *c.* 1915. This shop still exists and is easily identifiable on the right-hand side of the road at the top of Princes Street.

Albert Street is a continuation of Princes Street and runs in a generally north-north-easterly direction from the latter's junction with Victoria Street and Arbroath Road. This picture dates from 1918 but the buildings look just the same today. Beyond James C. Gow's grocer's shop on the left is St John the Baptist Episcopal Church and Hall with a date stone of 1893. Further along the street, the steeple of Stobswell Parish Church of Scotland rises above the chimney pots.

Balmore Street, viewed from its junction with Albert Street, looking towards Dura Street. It is notable because all the boys standing in the street are working for their living; one is washing down the pavement, another is crossing the road balancing a tray of pies on his head, while others are carrying packages for delivery somewhere – they were probably shopkeepers' errand boys. The four-storey buildings look just the same today, but the buildings on Dura Street have been replaced by the Dura Street/Catherine Street Car Park.

Stobswell was originally a small hamlet outside the city, built around a well which serviced the nearby farmhouses of Janefield and Maryfield. Housing was built in the area by the city's jute barons in the nineteenth century to accommodate workers in the textile mills in the area. A major road junction was constructed here, and in this picture the cameraman is standing in Dura Street. Mains Loan is on the left. The tramlines are running from Albert Street on the right, to begin the ascent of Forfar Road past the railings on the left. The road with the horse and cart approaching is Pitkerro Road, while Morgan Street goes off to the right past the wine merchant's shop in the tenement of Simpson Place.

John Morgan, the son of a Dundee maltster, emigrated to India aged twenty and became a very wealthy farmer. On his death in 1850 he bequeathed much of his fortune to establish a boarding school for the sons of artisans and tradesmen. The result was this building, which occupies a site between the Forfar and Pitkerro roads and opened in 1868 as the Morgan Hospital, a charitable institution which provided accommodation and education for 'sons of tradesmen and persons of the working class whose parents stand in the need of assistance'. In 1888 Morgan Hospital closed and was bought by the members of the Dundee Burgh Schools Board who reopened it the next year as the Morgan Academy. It ceased to be a boarding school and was redesigned to provide classroom accommodation for 650 pupils. It became a comprehensive in 1972. In 2001 the school suffered a serious fire which destroyed much of the building and only part of one wing of the quadrangular structure was saved. Fortunately, it was rebuilt using the original façade and reopened in 2004.

These houses, photographed around 1915, are situated in the area of Forfar Road known as Daisybank and are located opposite the west side of the Morgan Academy's grounds. The nearer house with its gable facing the road is 24 Forfar Road which was owned by Alexander Whyte, baker. Immediately behind the boys is Janefield Place leading off to the left and then follows the large three-storey house at number 26 which is nowadays divided into nine apartments.

The East Dundee Poorhouse was built on a 5-acre site off Mains Loan in 1854. It was designed to house 800 paupers, 100 sick people and 100 'lunatics', with men housed on one side of the building and women on the other; the central dining hall also served as a chapel. The buildings were enlarged and extended over the years and, in 1929, its running was taken over by the city council and it began to concentrate its efforts on maternity and child care. The hospital eventually occupied the whole of the old poorhouse site and was Dundee's second main hospital after the Royal Infirmary. After Ninewells Hospital was opened in 1972 it closed down to patients in 1976. Most of the buildings were demolished by 1990.

When Janet Keiller ran a small confectionery shop in Seagate in the 1760s she modified a quince recipe and produced marmalade. Her son James Keiller took over the business from 1797 and the firm assumed his name. Marmalade was just one of their product lines; the firm was a leader in butterscotch production, and other lines included jams, cakes and confectionery. James's son Alexander moved the premises to Castle Street in 1845 and introduced steam-powered machinery. In 1870 the firm moved into a factory in Albert Square but this burned down in 1900; it was rebuilt at a cost of £30,000 (about £3 million in today's money) and by 1920 the factory had 800 employees. The Albert Square factory was closed in 1947 (demolished in 1978) and relocated to Mains Loan, Maryfield. The Keiller brand was sold several times and its final owner from 1988 was Alma Holdings. They expanded the Mains Loan factory but went into receivership in 1992. The brand was sold on three more times but was eventually phased out and no longer exists. The buildings at Mains Loan were subsequently demolished.

Mid Mill was the premises of Cargill & Company on Pitkerro Road on the northern edge of Baxter Park. Cargill & Company bought the works from the Dundee Bank in 1854, building cottages and bothies for their workers. By 1867 it had 350 employees and in the Dundee Directory in 1897 the company was listed as bleachers, spinners and yarn merchants. In 1969 the company was bought out completely by William Watson (Dundee) Ltd but production at Mid Mill ended in 1980 with the loss of 70 jobs. The import of cheaper-priced carpets from abroad was blamed for the closure. There is now a school and acres of housing where Mid Mill once stood.

In 1853 the council leased a parcel of land at Stobsmuir, to the north-east of Baxter Park, and built two ponds. One became the Dundee Curling Club's curling pond and the other became a skating pond. For a time during the nineteenth century these ponds also acted as a trunk mains for the city's water supply but this was a very unsatisfactory arrangement; when a qualified water engineer was appointed in the 1870s he arranged the construction of proper reservoirs at Clatto and Lintrathen so that Dundonians had a decent water supply. A third pond was added in the 1870s, followed by a fourth later in the century. In 1909 the Dundee Curling Club moved to a new location off Forfar Road and the council then merged the two original ponds into one with an island in the middle. The third was drained and filled in to provide a recreation area and the fourth was retained for skating in the winter and model yachting in the summer. It was after these changes that swans were introduced, giving the ponds their local name of 'Swannie Ponds'. During the Second World War the ponds were filled in to prevent reflections that would provide a target for enemy aircraft, but following the war they were re-excavated.

This picture shows Park Avenue from its junction with Albert Street up to Baxter Park Terrace, with the gates of Baxter Park visible in the distance. The tower of the Park United Free Church is visible on the left-hand side of the road at its junction with Morgan Street. Note the coalman's cart just right of centre. He had to carry 1cwt (51 kilos) sacks of coal up two, three

and even four sets of twisting stairs, wearing protective gear of a solid-leather back-plate covering his lower neck and upper rump, and tied with straps over his shoulders and across his chest. This offered protection not only from knobbly coal lumps but also from the often rain-soaked hessian sacks.

The top end of Park Avenue at its junction with Baldovan Terrace. The view of Baxter Park at the top of the street is still the same today. The park was gifted to the people of Dundee by the Baxter family in 1863 and a part of its pavilion can be glimpsed through the trees.

The tenements on Park Avenue, Morgan Place and Baxter Park Terrace were all built in 1901 on what had been West Craigie Park. This had been laid out as a football ground and was home to Our Boys, forerunners of Dundee FC, and in existence from 1882 to 1893. It was Dundee FC's first pitch, but was used for only a few months before it was given up in favour of Caroline Port, after which it was taken over by Dundee Harp, precursors to Dundee United. This view of the corner of Baldovan Terrace and Park Avenue dates from 1920. The Park United Free church is visible to the right of the lamppost.

Park Avenue enters into Baxter Park Terrace from the left in this 1914 picture. This elegant terrace was built in the 1880s and its superior tenements and open outlook across the park have made it a sought-after address from the time it was built. The structure at the end of the road is part of Morgan Academy.

Baxter Park was donated to the citizens of the city by Sir David Baxter and his two sisters, Mary Ann and Eleanor. The land was acquired in 1861, on a site that was at the time on the edge of the city, and it was laid out at a cost of £40,000 (about £4 million today). Sir David intended that the park should afford to the working population 'the means of relaxation and enjoyment after their hard labour and honest industry'; after all, it was their hard labour that had made his family's fortune. A crowd of 70,000 gathered to watch the official opening in 1863. The park was laid out in two distinct parts; the northern

part as a pleasure garden composed of walks with open areas of grass and flower beds, the southern area as a parade ground. A large terrace, running east-west, linked the two parts. A pavilion was built in the middle of the park, with a marble life-size statue of Sir David standing under its canopy. In 1903 the Town Council took over its running and 100 years later it was granted £3.25 million through the Heritage Lottery Fund and underwent a £5 million refurbishment. It was reopened by HM Queen Elizabeth II in July 2007.

The Baxter Park pavilion was designed and built in 1859-63. It originally housed a restaurant at one end and a gardeners' room and ladies' room at the other. Later in the twentieth century the pavilion was closed and spent some years derelict. Fortunately, it was restored in the 1990s and is now used as an events and wedding venue. A café was incorporated in the west wing and a reception area/registry office opened in the east wing.

The bowling green at Baxter Park was opened by Provost Moncur in 1884. The cost was about £400, paid for by the Provost himself. In 1923 a new pavilion replaced the original one and this was extended in 1963. The houses in the background are on Wortley Place.

A 1930s photograph of Baxter Park bowling club members proudly displaying their competition trophies.

Arbroath Road, Dundee.

Eden Street on the right, and the trees in Baxter Park are on the left of this view of Arbroath Road.

Photographed around 1916, no trace now remains of these buildings, which were located just beyond the eastern end of Blackscroft as the whole area has been redeveloped with modern housing.

The Craigiebank housing scheme was the second estate to be built after Logie and half the number of houses had walls constructed of steel plate in the Caledon shipyard, erected on-site with the rivets showing through paint and render. The estate was planned in 1918 as a garden suburb. At its centre was to be a group of community buildings, including a church, a college, shops and sports facilities but in the event only Craigiebank Parish Church was built in 1938 (demolished in 2023). This picture shows Craigie Avenue which is a dual carriageway road that bisects the estate.

In 1947 the U.K. Time Company (a subsidiary of the US Time Corporation) opened its Milton and Camperdown factories in Dundee. Milton had 60% male employees and predominantly produced tools and components while Camperdown was 80% female and did the assembly work. In 1957 the company changed its name to Timex and its workforce peaked in 1974 at around 6,000, when it was the largest domestic supplier of watches to the UK market and exported 90% of its production. The advent of digital watches marked the end of watchmaking in Dundee and the firm diversified into manufacturing Polaroid and Nimslo 3-D cameras and later gained a contract with Sinclair Research to manufacture (with a reduced workforce and the Milton site closed) its personal computing products, principally the ZX81 and the ZX Spectrum models. However, in 1986 Sir Clive Sinclair's computer business was bought out by Amstrad who ended the contract with Timex. Timex then tried to lay off workers, leading to a long and bitter industrial relations dispute, and the Camperdown factory eventually closed in 1993.

THE ASSOCIATION OF JUTE SPINNERS & MANUFACTURERS

Dundee and District is the only Manufacturing Centre of Jute in Britain. Jute's uses are almost legion and without Jute few industries can operate efficiently.

THE LARGEST EMPLOYER OF LABOUR IN THE CITY

Of the Natural Textile Industries, the Jute Industry is the most up-to-date in equipment and machinery. In spite of this fact, plans for even greater improvement of such plant, of working conditions, and of the products of the Trade, are being put into action by every firm. Research is playing a prominent part in the future planning of the Jute Industry, and a British Jute Trade Research Association has been formed, embracing all sections of the Industry including Textile Machinery Makers as well as Dyers.

JUTE HAS A GREAT PAST — AND A GREATER FUTURE

THOMAS C. KEAY, LTD.
Engineers
DUNDEE

Makers of
Sack Printing Machines—Single or Multi-colour
Cloth Lapping and Cutting Machines
"Duralip" Bobbins for High Speed Gill Spinning Frames
Loom Pickers   Loom Shuttles, etc.

Works   Regd. Office
DENSFIELD WORKS   **15 BALTIC STREET**

LAWSIDE ENGINEERING AND FOUNDRY COMPANY LIMITED
Textile Engineers and Ironfounders

Makers of Jute Openers, Softeners, Dressing, Beaming, Weaving, and Finishing Machinery

Regd. Office and Works
**LAWSIDE FOUNDRY
DUNDEE**

Edward McGregor, Ltd.
ST. ANDREWS CONFECTIONERY WORKS

Telephones 6112-6113   **DON'S ROAD**   Telegraphic Address
                        DUNDEE   "Bon-Bons"

Makers of fine confections
for home and export

BOILED SWEETS, MINT & FRUIT IMPERIALS,
LOZENGES, CARAMELS, CANDIES ETC.

Upper left: At the turn of the twentieth century the jute industry was booming and this Association's assertion of an even greater future for the industry seemed realistic. But already the writing was on the wall because by 1914 it had become cheaper to import the finished product from India. The manufacturing industry gradually declined so that from over half the population of Dundee being employed in jute manufacture and its associated industries in more than 130 factories in 1900, the proportion had declined to 18.5% by 1951. Commercial production of jute had virtually ended in the city in the 1970s; the last of the jute spinners, Tay Spinners, ceased production in 1998.

Upper right: Adverts by two of Dundee's specialist engineering firms. Lawside Engineering & Foundry Company Ltd was a wholly-owned subsidiary of Thomas C. Keay Ltd. Lack of business caused the Lawside factory to be closed in 1971 when the various activities there were transferred to Densfield Works. In April 1977 the company went into receivership. Attempts to find a buyer were unsuccessful and the plant and machinery at Densfield Works were auctioned off.

Left: An advert from the 1950s.

This is an advert from the 1950s, judging by the styles.

The port of Dundee is thought to have existed since the eleventh century. It really started to grow in the early nineteenth century and improvement works were begun in 1815. The King William IV Dock was opened in 1825, the Earl Grey Dock in 1834, the Camperdown Dock in 1865 and the Victoria Dock and East Graving Dock in 1875. By the 1890s ships were becoming too large to fit into the walled docks so the Eastern Wharf was built. Railways had been at the docks since the 1830s and by 1933 there were 14 miles of track. The King William IV Dock, Earl Grey Dock and the Tidal Basin were all filled in during the construction of the Tay Road Bridge in the 1960s.

A note on the back of this undated photograph says 'H.L.I. + Womens' Army Auxiliary Corps'. The location is unidentified but is believed to be in the Dundee area. This Corps was formally instituted in 1917 to free up more men to go on active service. More than 57,000 women served, mainly as drivers, cooks, and clerks. The Corps was disbanded in 1921.

This company was founded by William Rettie and James Low in 1868. The name consists of both the founders' names, one's first name and the other's surname. James's brother, William, joined the firm in 1870 and took over running the business some years later. Popularly referred to as 'Willie Low's', the company expanded to become a nationwide chain of supermarkets until it was bought out by Tesco in 1994. Its main offices were at 22-36 Blackness Road, now demolished.

In 1927 the *St Andrews Citizen* reported that 'Much has been achieved by the band in the cause of charity, and it is well known in Dundee that since its inception in 1919 the band has, through various means, raised upwards of £3,000 for local charities. This is the only known Masonic Pipe Band.' Camperdown Masonic Lodge 317 still exists but not so the pipe band, of which there is no apparent mention in the newspapers after 1928.

This 28-seater Leyland charabanc named 'Greyhound' was registered to Dickson Brothers of Graham Street, Dundee, in 1922. The company advertised in the *Dundee Courier*: 'Charabancs De Luxe for hire, 18 and 28 seaters; also round trips from Albert Square, Wednesday and Saturday, starting 2.30pm., 4.0, 6.30 and 8pm., number of passengers permitting. Fares 1s 3d, 1s 6d and 2s.'

These three happy assistants in a Dundee confectionery shop are standing behind a mouth-watering selection of cakes.

The full crates of bottles behind them and the empty crates they are sitting on suggest that these workmen are in the cobbled yard of a brewery.

Tram No. 63, built in 1907, offered the driver very little protection from the elements. Tramcar crews comprised a driver and conductor who were issued with heavy-duty, double-breasted greatcoats and peaked caps. These uniforms must have been very necessary in the midst of Dundee winters.

POST CARD.

FINEST SELECTED SHEEP CASING, BEECH CHOPPING BLOCKS, ETC. CHEAPEST IN THE TRADE.

MINCERS, FILLERS, SCALES, CUTLERY, MOTORS AND SAFES. ALL IN STOCK.

HARRY BELL,

Complete Butchers' Outfitter,

Gut and Spice Merchant,

14 Ferry Road,

DUNDEE.

Harry Bell appears to have opened this Aladdin's Cave of a shop at 14 Ferry Road (now Broughty Ferry Road) in 1924.

During 1937 Harry expanded into the newly-vacated premises next door at number 16, which is when this photograph was taken, and he even had a third address at 28 Broughty Ferry Road until the early 1940s before reverting just to his shop at 14-16 Broughty Ferry Road.